Follow the Light

How God Reveals Himself through Light

JULIE GARRO

WESTBOW
P R E S S®
A DIVISION OF THOMAS NELSON
& ZONDERVAN

WestBow Press books may be ordered through booksellers or by contacting:

WestBow Press
A Division of Thomas Nelson & Zondervan
1663 Liberty Drive
Bloomington, IN 47403
www.westbowpress.com
1 (866) 928-1240

Because of the dynamic nature of the Internet, any web addresses or links contained in this book may have changed since publication and may no longer be valid. The views expressed in this work are solely those of the author and do not necessarily reflect the views of the publisher, and the publisher hereby disclaims any responsibility for them.

Any people depicted in stock imagery provided by Thinkstock are models, and such images are being used for illustrative purposes only.
Certain stock imagery © Thinkstock.

ISBN: 978-1-4908-9811-7 (sc)
ISBN: 978-1-4908-9812-4 (e)

Library of Congress Control Number: 2015917905

Print information available on the last page.

WestBow Press rev. date: 01/07/2016

Acknowledgements

Thank you to Rev. Jackie Gause, Rev. Sharon Reid, Jessica, Glenda, Ellie, Teresa, Lyn, Mary, Joy, Evelyn, and Marjorie, for all their love and support in making this study possible, and Rabbi Ralph Mecklenberger for pointing me to the details.

Dedication

To all those who follow God's light.
Shine that light so brightly that darkness is not even a memory.

Contents

Introduction

Everyone has experienced the ups and downs of life. After a particularly trying time in my life, I wanted to understand that experience better and become closer to God. To learn more about Him, I chose to read the entire Bible again. This is an exercise many Christians go through to ensure they spend adequate time in God's Holy Word. Some even attempt to read the Bible in one year. It is a great exercise and I have been blessed when I have done it. However, we do not need to speed-read the Bible. Meditating on a particular section of Scripture is also a fine way to study the Bible and spend precious time in God's Word. It is when I devote time reflecting on one passage that I see new truths I have missed before. I believe God is speaking to my heart and I am excited and am drawn even closer to my Lord. So this time I did not set a time limit to complete reading the Bible. I chose to slow down and earnestly study the Scriptures. Little did I know that God would touch my heart on the first page of Genesis!

The Bible study you are holding is a result of my "conversation" with the Lord and the adventure He took me on through the pages of Scripture. As a result of this journey, I fell in love with my Savior all over again. God presented me with a theme, another way to be overwhelmed by His greatness. Then, He took me on a tour of His Holy Word in an extraordinary way, and opened my eyes to truths I never noticed before. My prayer is you will let yourself be truly amazed as you study God's word and listen to our Heavenly Father speak to your heart also.

Each week of the first seven weeks of this study are divided into five daily assignments. These assignments should take about fifteen to twenty minutes to complete each day. There is also a suggested prayer topic to close each day's assignment. Along the way I have noted some Bible verses you may want to commit to memory. The final "week" of this study is designed for personal reflection and prayer. It contains more than fifty prayer topics. You may consider journaling your prayers in a separate notebook.

As you work through this Bible study you will visit many books of the Bible, by design. The Bible is one book, but It is also a library of sixty-six separate books woven together by common themes. If you eagerly study the Scriptures, you will find you want to know more, and God will show you more. Our Creator will excite you and bless you as you learn His extraordinary ways.

All Scripture quoted in this Bible study is from the New International Version (NIV) unless otherwise noted. Studying Scripture is often enhanced by consulting a second version of the Bible. Consider picking up a copy of the Amplified Version, English Standard Version (ESV), The Message Version (MSG), or another version to aid in your study and discovery.

"This is the message we have heard from Him and declare to you: God is light; in Him there is no darkness at all." 1 John 1:5

WEEK ONE

In The Beginning

Day One

Documenting

"This is what the Lord, the God of Israel, says: 'Write in a book all the words I have spoken to you.'" Jeremiah 30:2

The destination is not always the best part of the journey. Sometimes it is those stops along the way that once we look back, are the best part of the entire experience. Being in a new culture or seeing something for the first time can provide clarity and open our minds to new possibilities. Those special, out-of-the-way moments are often the ones that change us the most. If we had not been in a specific place, at a certain time, a significant event may never have occurred; we would not be changed.

I went sightseeing many times when I was stationed at Kadena Air Force Base, Okinawa, Japan. One sunny afternoon I was exploring a rocky beach, while taking as many pictures as the Japanese. When I returned to the base, I realized I had lost my wallet during that hike. A few days later, my wallet showed up at the main gate to the base. When I retrieved it, I was delighted to find it wrapped in a letter that introduced the fisherman who found it, and his children—who wanted to practice their English skills, by the way. I had the opportunity to thank the man for returning my wallet, and I also enjoyed several conversations with his children. An afternoon of exploration and a lost wallet gave me the opportunity to experience the Japanese culture on a level I would have otherwise missed.

We document our lives with photographs and journals. We remember birthdays, graduations, weddings, holidays, and vacations through pictures and other memorabilia. We do not realize how far we have come until we look at those photographs and other mementos. The same holds true with our spiritual journey. We study, share, learn,

3

and grow. There is biblical precedence for documenting; it is a way to help us learn. Documenting helps us track our progress. The Israelites kept God's Word close to them so they could memorize it, and learn from it. Look at what Deuteronomy tells us.

> "Hear, O Israel: The Lord our God, the Lord is one. Love the Lord your God with all your heart and with all your soul and with all your strength. These commandments that I give you today are to be on your hearts. Impress them on your children. Talk about them when you sit at home and when you walk along the road, when you lie down and when you get up. Tie them as symbols on your hands and bind them on your foreheads. *Write* them on the doorframes of your houses and on your gates." Deuteronomy 6:4-9 (italics added).

Record the following verses in the space provided.

Proverbs 7:3

Deuteronomy 27:8

Isaiah 8:1

Jeremiah 31:33

Luke 1:3

1 John 1:4

What do all these verses have in common?

Circle, or highlight the word *write* in each of the verses above. Here we see biblical precedence for documenting.

Document the beginning of our journey with an exercise. Fold a blank sheet of paper in half. On one-half of the page write the word *light*. Now write down everything that comes to mind when you think of that word. On the other side of the paper, write the word *God*. What comes to mind when you think of God? What words would you use to describe God, Jesus, and the Holy Spirit?

Review the two lists. What words are similar?

Jot down your immediate thoughts about the comparisons.

Keep this list handy throughout this study. As we journey through God's marvelous Word, you may find additional descriptions and definitions you will want to add to your lists.

Write a prayer asking God to illuminate your heart
and speak to you through His Holy Scriptures.

Day Two

First Words

"And God said, 'Let there be light,' and there was light." Genesis 1:3

Science is fascinating to me. I am mesmerized by programs on Animal Planet and by National Geographic specials. Narrators explain nature, physics, and astronomy in lay terms. As I watch these programs I am reminded of how incredibly creative and intelligent our God is. He made our world so intriguing and complex we are still discovering its mysteries. Several branches of science and thousands of years of discovery have given us significant information, yet the complete knowledge of many phenomena simply eludes us. No one person can begin to understand everything.

Even more fascinating is that there is still more to be discovered. God created our world in such a way that we would desire to seek Him. I take you on this journey as a fellow student looking for answers from Scripture (Jeremiah 33:3). I will reference some scientific facts along the way as we look at how God has revealed Himself to us through His marvelous creation. Shall we get started?

―――――

Meditate on a portion of the creation story: Genesis 1:1-19. Part of the passage is reprinted below.

> God made two great lights—the greater light to govern the day and the lesser light to govern the night. He also made the stars. God set them in the vault of the sky to give light on the earth, to govern the day and the night, and to

separate light from darkness. And God saw that it was good. And there was evening, and there was morning—the fourth day. Genesis 1:16-19

What? Back up! God did not make the sun, moon, and stars until the fourth day of creation? What was the light on the first day of creation? Go back and read just verses 1-5.

What were the first words God spoke in Genesis?

What did God say about the light?

What else did God make on the first day?

Review the entire creation story (Genesis 1:1-2:3). What do you think is important in God's order of creation?

Do we know anything else about *the beginning?* Study John 1:1-13. Who else was present in the beginning?

When did He exist?

What was coming into the world?

Are there similarities between the opening of Genesis and the first few verses of the gospel of John? Juxtapose Genesis 1:1-5 with John 1:1-5, 9.

Genesis 1:1-5
In the beginning God created the heavens and the earth. Now the earth was formless and empty, darkness was over the surface of the deep, and the Spirit of God was hovering over the waters.

John 1:1-5, 9
In the beginning was the Word, and the Word was with God, and the Word was God. He was with God in the beginning. Through him all things were made; without him nothing was made that has

And God said, "Let there be light," and there was light. God saw that the light was good, and he separated the light from the darkness. God called the light "day," and the darkness he called "night." And there was evening, and there was morning—the first day.

been made. In him was life, and that life was the light of all mankind. The light shines in the darkness, and the darkness has not overcome it.

. . .

The true light that gives light to everyone was coming into the world.

Do you see the Holy Trinity in any of these verses? In the passages above, circle or highlight the words describing the persons of the Holy Trinity. Using a different color, circle or highlight the word *light*. What do you notice?

The metaphor *light*, is used to describe our Savior. This metaphor is used early in the life of Jesus. Mary and Joseph took Jesus to present Him at the temple on the eighth day, as required by Jewish law and tradition. In Luke 2:25-32 we find Simeon, a righteous and devout man, enlightened by God. Simeon took Jesus in his arms and praised God. How does Simeon describe the baby Jesus?

What does Luke 2:25-32 reveal to you about how God uses *light* as a metaphor?

What do the following verses tell you about the various ways God wants to be perceived?

Psalm 76:4

Psalm 89:15

Psalm 104:2

Psalm 118:27

Psalm 139:12

Turn to the end of the Bible, to Revelation. In the last chapters, we get a glimpse of the New Jerusalem, our heavenly home. Look at Revelation 21:22–27 and 22:3–6. What will God give?

Where will the light come from?

Light is a metaphor for God, and it is used throughout Scripture. Imagine no darkness at all, just the pure and radiant light of God! I look forward to feasting my eyes on that perfect light one day. Record 1 John 1:5 here and consider committing the verse to memory.

Our Heavenly Father begins, ends, and sprinkles the Holy Scriptures with references to *light*. In fact, the word *light* is used more than two hundred times in the Bible. The first words God spoke were "Let there be light." *Light* is an important metaphor for God, because it is one way to describe His attributes (see the exercise on day one). The Bible is full of facts and the occasional difficult concept. A metaphor helps us understand God because the metaphor explains or describes a specific, complex concept using an easy to understand idea. Did God open His Holy Word with both fact and metaphor?

I believe God wanted it to be easy to get to know Him. Light is a way for God to reveal Himself to us. Therefore, on the first day of creation God said, "Let there be light." Then He spoke everything else into existence.

Write a prayer thanking God for creation and for His
plans to make Himself known to man.

Day Three

What is Light?

"Happy are the people who know how to praise You. Lord, let them live in the light of Your presence." Psalm 89:15 (NCV)

We are fascinated by the various ways our world is lit up. Lamps, fireworks, neon lights, fire light, and Christmas lights are a few of the ways light enters our lives. We expect light to be there for us. We trust the sun will rise, we expect lights to come on in our homes and businesses, and we trust the moon and stars to light up the night. We need light, but do we truly know what light is?

Much of science is based on theory. We cannot prove the concept. Instead, scientists study how the element, animal or phenomena behaves, and then develop a theory to explain that behavior. They determine a theory is true based on, in part, observation. When scientists discover the properties that do not change, the theory becomes *fact*. To properly study *light* we must study how light behaves. In the same way, we learn about our great God by observing the way He behaves. Once we get to know our God, we realize God's nature does not change.

List some of the ways you know God is unchanging.

Do the steadfast qualities of God provide you comfort? Why?

Now we turn our attention to light. What is light? Can you define it?

Is there a reason why we cannot completely understand light? It is possible we are not meant to. There are other things we are not allowed to understand completely, or even see—at least this side of heaven. Turn to Exodus 33:18-23 and read about Moses and the glory of the Lord.

Moses was allowed to see what part of God?

What part of God must not be seen?

Moses had a deep, intimate relationship with God, yet he was only allowed to see God's back. I imagine Moses yearning to see God's face, just as we do. There are some details we will have to wait for heaven to see. Why?

God gives us an answer in Isaiah 55:8. What does this verse tell us?

While God's thoughts are not our thoughts, and His ways are not our ways, He has revealed Himself through His splendid creation. That creation includes light.

The Science of Light and Color

Now stick with me through the following technical jargon and remember who created science in the first place. I promise you will be rewarded for your diligence.

Visible light is part of the electromagnetic (EM) spectrum. This spectrum is radiation and is divided into types of waves. EM radiation carries energy, called photons.[1] The waves we can see are visible light and are between certain frequencies near the middle of the EM spectrum. Each frequency is a different color. In 1670, Sir Isaac Newton demonstrated that white light is composed of all the colors of the spectrum by refracting sunlight through a prism.[2]

White light is the presence of all color. That idea sounds backward, but I remember my eleventh grade physics teacher proving this concept to us. She placed red, yellow, and blue cellophane over the lenses of three projectors. We could see three different colored circles. Then she moved the projectors so all the colors came together—the light was white.[3]

Light is the exclusive source of color in the world. When light disappears, color fades.[4] Colors are made of wavelengths. When we see colors we see the wavelengths of light that are not absorbed by the object.[5] Black is the absence of color,[6] or the absence of light.

Why do you think God provided us color?

When we think of light, the first thing we think of is usually white light, from a light bulb, street light, or the sun. White light is more than illumination, it is also color. Why is this relevant? The Bible discusses white, and color, in several places. What colors and objects are described in each of these passages, and how are the objects relevant?

Genesis 1:30

Exodus 26:14

Exodus 26:31-32

Exodus 28:1-5

1 Chronicles 29:2-4

Revelation 21:19-21

Mark 9:3

Revelation 20:11

Color is associated with holy objects, but our creative God colored our world when He created it. A black, white, and gray world would have been enough, but enough is not enough for our great God. He blessed us with light and color. He planned this treat for our eyes from the beginning of creation so we would have a glimpse of heaven, and grasp how creative and generous He is.

Sight

When I was in the fifth grade, I had to get eyeglasses. I could not see to the front of the classroom without squinting. I was devastated at being called "four-eyes," but the truth is, I could see clearly with the eyeglasses. The ability to see begins when light enters your eyes.[7] If you are in a dark room and you turn on the light you can see more clearly. Without the gift of light, sight would be meaningless. Without light, there would be no sight.

What do the following verses tell us about God's miraculous gift of sight?

Genesis 1:26-27

Exodus 4:11

Psalm 146:8

Luke 18:42

God created sight and gave it to us as a gift. To enjoy sight we also depend on God's gift of light.

How Light Travels

Light travels very quickly, 186,282 miles per second.[8] The photons of light travel in a straight line, until blocked. Light is coming to us in the fastest and most direct way possible—that is a straight line.[9] God is available to us in the fastest and most direct way possible too—with just a prayer.

Write a prayer thanking God for light, color and sight.

Day Four

Shadows

"Every good and perfect gift is from above, coming down from the Father of the heavenly lights, who does not change like shifting shadows." James 1:17

When our teachers turned on projectors and white light was cast toward the front of the classroom, there was always someone who would make shadow figures with his hands, usually a dog, or a bird. The image that was cast was a fair representation of the real thing. We knew exactly what the boy was trying to make with his hands, but it was not real.

A shadow is an artificial image created by an object that blocks light. A shadow is a two dimensional image, without color. Shadows can be frightening, but we should remember light is necessary for a shadow to be cast. In the context of Scripture, our earthly existence is only a shadow of what is to come when we reach heaven. What do the following verses tell us about shadows?

Colossians 2:17

Hebrews 8:5

Hebrews 10:1

Write Matthew 4:16 here.

What does *The Shadow of Death* mean in this verse?

What does *The Shadow of Death* mean in Psalm 23:4 (NASB)?

One answer may be found in the second chapter of Revelation. "I see where you live, right under the shadow of Satan's throne. But you continue boldly in my Name; you never once denied my Name, even when the pressure was worst, when they martyred Antipas, my witness who stayed faithful to me on Satan's turf." Revelation 2:13 (MSG)

When the apostle John wrote Revelation, Pergamos was an important religious center for several pagan cults, and the Greek god Zeus. On the acropolis in Pergamos was a huge, throne-shaped altar to Zeus.[10] The parallels to today's culture are numerous. Many people are engaging in false religions, are worshipping false prophets, and have found or made modern-day idols to bow down to.

According to Revelation 2:13, where do we live?

According to this verse, how did the Pergamums respond?

How should we respond?

In order for shadows to be cast, light must be present. Do you find comfort in this knowledge? Why?

Despite what happens in our world, God is always in control of our circumstances. Write the following verses here and consider committing them to memory.

Proverbs 19:21

Romans 8:28

1 Corinthians 10:13

No matter what the situation, or how difficult the circumstance seems to be, our great God is in control. Nothing will thwart His purposes.

Write a prayer thanking God for keeping you
in the palm of His Hand.

Legacy of Light

*"But the plans of the Lord stand firm forever, the purposes
of His heart through all generations." Psalm 33:11*

My sister-in-law is an accomplished photographer. She will tell you how important lighting is to every photograph. It takes patience to set the lights for the perfect portrait. Outdoor photography takes even longer. The time of day and angle of the sun must be considered. The season also plays an important role in how the light will enter the camera and touch the overall image. A photographer must wait for the right time to take a certain photograph. Take a look at the cover of this book. The light came through the trees at just the right time, and just the right angle, to produce this beautiful photograph. It could not have occurred on a cloudy day. God's work in our lives takes proper timing as well.

Timing is everything. What do the following Scriptures tell us about time?

Ecclesiastes 3:1

Zephaniah 3:20

1 Peter 5:6 (consider committing this verse to memory)

God's master plan requires we wait on Him. Learn patience and see what God will do with your life (Galatians 5:22; Colossians 3:12).

Light: Past, Present, and Future

Theoretically, light is coming from the past and goes into the future. Scientists have calculated the speed of light as 186,282 miles per second. Our sun is an average 93,000,000 miles away (the earth travels in a slight elliptical orbit).[11] Once you do the math you discover it takes about eight minutes and eighteen seconds for light from the sun to reach the earth. The light we see from the sun is eight minutes old.[12] The light that came from the past is sent into the future to light your today. God is infinite. His love, His light, is coming from the past into the future to prepare for us a today full of His love. He created a marvelous plan for us in the past, and sent it to the future for us to experience today.

Your parents or grandparents may have been instrumental in passing their faith on to you. They shared and sent their light into the future, from the past. You can send your light on to future generations. How has someone from your past sent the love of Christ forward to you?

Think ahead to the future, to your grandchildren, and their children. How are you going to send your light forward? How do you want to be remembered?

One of my most treasured possessions is my great-grandmother's Bible. It is one of the few possessions she had when she left Ireland and traveled by ship to America in 1898. With a broken spine and tattered pages, the Bible really is falling apart. But it represents the hopes, dreams, and courage God gave her to build a life in this new land for future generations. Once she arrived in America, she married and had eleven children. She went to heaven in 1950, but not before she left a godly legacy. In many ways, she sent her light ahead to me, and to my children.

How can you impact future generations?

What do the following verses tell us about our past and our future?

Isaiah 46:10

Jeremiah 29:11

Close your eyes for a moment. Think about the spiritual legacy you want to pass on. On a blank sheet of paper, write your eulogy, based on what you believe God has created you for.

Write a prayer thanking God for sending His light to you and ask Him to give you the wisdom and courage to pass His light onto future generations.

Special Section

A Study of the Word Light

Words are powerful; they are able to communicate thoughts and ideas as well as more tangible pieces of information. However, when we try to translate words from one language to another something often gets lost in the translation. My husband was raised in Spain. He often refers to Spanish words and phrases to explain a particular idea. He will try for several minutes to communicate the nuances of a language that does not make sense to a novice. After a time he will say, "There is no exact translation." Another example of the differences in languages is the Greek language has several different words to express various forms of love. *Phila* is brotherly love, *eros* is passion, *storge* is parental love, and *agape* is Christ's love.[13] The English language is different. *Love* is one word used to express all these different emotions.

When we study Scripture we are not reading original translations. Understanding the meaning of the original word can breathe additional depth and meaning into a passage, or even a phrase. The Old Testament was written in Hebrew; it makes sense to begin our study there. Depending on which dictionary you consult, a dictionary of the English language contains thirty-seven definitions of the word *light*. Our Bible was not written in English. If we refer to the original Hebrew and Greek translations, we find nineteen Hebrew entries for the word *light* and seventeen Greek entries.[14]

Consult several Bible commentaries discussing the creation story and you will find the word *light* in Genesis 1:3 is the Hebrew word *owr*. There are eleven meanings of the word, including *light of life* and *Jehovah as Israel's light*.[15] The MacArthur Bible Commentary explains *light* as meaning, "That which most clearly reveals and most closely approximates God's glory."[16] Use that sentence in place of the word *light* in Genesis 1:3 and we learn, "And God said, 'Let there be that which most clearly reveals and most closely approximates God's glory,' and there was that which most clearly reveals and most closely approximates God's glory." Remember this thought with the following word equation:

Light = That which most clearly reveals and most closely approximates God's glory.

What does *glory* mean? An excellent word picture is found in Exodus 40:34 (GNT). "Then the cloud covered the Tent and the dazzling light of the Lord's presence filled it." In this context, *glory* means "the weight or worthiness of something. It describes greatness and splendor, and it is sometimes translated as 'honor.'"[17] Our word equation looks like this:

Glory = Worthiness, greatness, splendor, and honor.

In the Strong's Bible Dictionary, *glory* also means *owr* or *light*.[18] Now our word equation looks like this:

Glory = Light.

In Genesis 1:3 when God said, "Let there be light," He was providing *His* glory, or Himself, as the light! This makes sense because God created man to fellowship with Him. There was no reason for God to withhold His very best. We can rewrite our word equation as:

Light = God.

In John 8:12, Jesus tells us He is the light of the world. John 14:10 tells us God and Jesus are one. The author of Hebrews tells us, "God's Son has all the brightness of God's own glory and is like him in every way. By His own mighty word, He holds the universe together. After the Son had washed away our sins, He sat down at the right side of the glorious God in heaven." Hebrews 1:3 (CEV)

The Greek word for *glory* is *doxa*. Doxa means "splendor, brightness, and a most glorious condition or exalted state. It also means "the glorious condition of blessedness into which is appointed and promised that Christians shall enter upon their Savior's return from heaven."[19]

The Son is not just reflecting God's glory; He is God and radiates His own essential glory.[20] This glory is sent forth and promised to true Christians after Christ's return.[21]

"He came to Jesus at night and said, 'Rabbi, we know that You are a teacher who has come from God. For no one could perform the signs You are doing if God were not with Him." John 3:2

WEEK TWO

The Leadership of Light

Day One

Follow the Leader

*"For this God is our God for ever and ever; He will
be our guide even to the end." Psalm 48:14*

When I was in boot camp my unit marched everywhere. Marching was an efficient and organized way of moving our unit from one location to the next. The key to marching in formation was following the leader, or our *guidon bearer*. The guidon bearer held the unit's flag, was always the most visible person in the unit, and was always in front of the formation. The guidon, or flag, represented the unit, and always stayed with the unit. In years gone by the guidon was also a weapon.

Review Exodus 13:20-22. When the Israelites left Egypt how did God appear?

Why did God appear in these forms?

According to Exodus 13:22, when did the pillar leave the people?

What did the cloud do in Exodus 14:19-20?

God was the Israelites guidon. All the people had to do was follow the pillar of a cloud or pillar of fire. The cloud and fire represented more to the Israelites than a guide. The pillar represented God's observable presence with His people. In addition to guiding the Israelites, the pillar was protection and a visible identification of who the Israelites were, and who they belonged to.

Is God your guidon? What identifies you as a child of God?

More to the Story

The parting of the Red Sea is one of the most famous miracles in the Exodus story, but consider other portions of the narrative. Take a look at Exodus 14:19-20 again. What did the cloud do to the Egyptians?

What did the same cloud provide to the Israelites?

This cloud from God did something else in Exodus 19:9, 16-19. What did the cloud do?

Not only did the cloud provide guidance and protection, it spoke! (A cloud also spoke in Mark 9:7). In Exodus 20, the Lord was in the cloud when He gave Moses the Ten Commandments.

God spoke to Moses on several occasions, often giving him instructions. What does God ask the people to make in Exodus 25:8?

Why does God request this item?

God intended to dwell with His people. He gave Moses specific instructions for building a Tabernacle, so He would have a place to dwell (Exodus 26-31). The Tabernacle was completed in Exodus 40. What happened in Exodus 40:34-38? (The same event is documented in Leviticus 9:23-24.)

Our study of the word *light* (previous section) showed us the glory of the Lord is *light*. God's glory, God's light, filled the Tabernacle.

In Leviticus 16:2, how does God say He will appear?

In what ways does God appear to the Israelites in Exodus 40:34-38?

During their time in the wilderness, God was visibly present with His people. He appeared as a cloud and a pillar of fire (Exodus 13:21), as fire on Mount Sinai (Exodus 19:18), and as a cloud over the Tabernacle (Exodus 40:34-38). In his book, The Shekinah Glory, George L. Miller explains the visible manifestation of God and the presence of God is known as the *Shekinah*.[22] The word *Shekinah* is not in the Bible, but the word *Trinity* is not in the Bible either. However, the Bible teaches the principles of the Trinity, and that we worship one God, presented as three distinct personalities. *Shekinah* is the Hebrew word to express the presence of God on earth.[23]

The first reference to God leading the Israelites as a pillar of fire or a cloud is in Exodus 13:21. The last reference to the Lord appearing in this form is near the end of Moses' life, recorded in Deuteronomy 31:15, when God brought the Israelites to the edge of the Promised Land. The Lord was visibly present with the Israelites for forty years. Light, in its many forms, is a similar reminder of the presence of God in our daily lives.

In the New Testament, we find Jesus with the same attributes found in the God of the Old Testament. Write Colossians 2:9 here.

How does Jesus describe Himself in John 8:12?

Write a prayer thanking God for His constant presence and guidance in your life.

Day Two

On a Mountainside

"Now when Jesus saw the crowds, He went up on a mountainside and sat down. His disciples came to Him, and He began to teach them." Matthew 5:1-2

The Bible is the Word of God. It is also literature. One of the ways to study the Bible is to study passages based on the literary form in which they were written. The sixty-six books that make up the Bible contain numerous literary forms such as poetry, history, allegories, and parables, to name a few. Jesus often taught using parables because parables were dramatized stories from everyday life that people would recognize and understand. Parables also revealed a new spiritual truth. Today, our understanding of a concept or spiritual truth can be much richer by meditating on a particular passage and reading it in the full context of God's Holy Word, and the literary form it is presented in.

Light was a theme Jesus used often in His parables. This part of our journey takes place where Jesus delivered The Sermon on the Mount. Immediately after Jesus delivers the Beatitudes, we learn about salt and light. Study Matthew 5:13-16.

In verse 14 Jesus states, "You are the _____ of the world." This is a statement of fact; we are seen. Everything we do is visible to others. Jesus was also explaining that we are to be light for more than the immediate community; we are to be light for everyone, even the Gentiles. This was a radical concept to the Jews who believed for centuries that they were the chosen people.

How do you shine your light into the world? (What is your spiritual gift?) Discuss this question with your small group.

Who do you shine your light for?

Are you shining your light for a select group of people? Why?

What do you think Jesus wants us to understand from verse 14?

Verse 16 states: "Let your _____ shine before others." What is the difference between verse 14 and verse 16?

How does James 2:17 relate to Matthew 5:16?

Do you believe Matthew 5:13-16 is a command directed at you? Why or why not?

Verse 15 may hold the answer. "Neither do people light a lamp and put it under a bowl. Instead they put it on its stand, and it gives light to everyone in the house." This verse commands us to share the light of God with others. All others.

How can you be sure you are sharing your light?

We cannot live according to the ways of this world and be an effective disciple. We must actively share our faith. Our culture has made discussing our faith taboo, except with other Christians. However, failure to share the love of Christ is to disobey God's

Word (Matthew 28:16–20). There are many ways to show and share our faith. We need to consider who we come in contact with every day. Who can we share the light of Christ with?

Later in the sermon, Jesus discusses the light of the body and the eye. Read Matthew 6:22–23 and paraphrase the verses. (You may want to consult other versions of the Bible.)

What differences do you learn from reading another version?

What do these verses tell you about living in today's world?

I must admit how much I like my possessions, as do most Americans. Go ahead, admit it. I am also cynical about the motives of anyone I do not know, so I do not help some people that maybe I should. While we must be wise, we must also use every opportunity to be the window to God for everyone we meet, especially to those we may want to distrust. I must remember that it is not up to me to determine the worthiness of the person I am helping; I am just to be Christ for him or her.

List some ways to keep your spiritual life healthy.

Write a prayer asking God to help you open your heart to the lost world.

Day Three

Parables

"After this, Jesus traveled about from one town and village
to another, proclaiming the good news of the Kingdom
of God. The Twelve were with him." Luke 8:1

Our Lord used His time wisely. When an opportunity arose to teach, He took that opportunity to deliver a spiritual truth. One night a Pharisee named Nicodemus came to Jesus. During this exchange Jesus gives us the most famous verse in the Bible, John 3:16. Read John 3:1-21. Note the phrases that use the word *light* and explain the metaphors Jesus was using.

What does Jesus mean by the phrase, *born again*?

Can you explain to a non-believer what it means to be *born again*? What would you tell him or her?

Focus on verses 19-21. How many times did Jesus use the word *light* in these three verses?

Jesus wanted us to understand He is the light.

In Luke's gospel we see Jesus delivering more parables. Summarize Luke 8:16-18.

This spiritual truth needed some reinforcement. Take a look at how Jesus expands on this lesson in another parable. Read Luke 11:33. How does this verse compare to the parable we just read?

I have many dear friends who teach. They will tell you it is important to introduce a concept, and build upon that concept with additional information. They often repeat themselves to drive home particular ideas. Jesus is a teacher. In this parable we see the Rabbi using lessons from previous parables, reinforcing important points.

Record the parable in Luke 11:35-36 here.

What is the main point of this teaching?

Compare these parables to the other parables we studied yesterday.

Why do you think Jesus repeated certain concepts?

Sharing our light is being fruitful. Jesus taught us to be fruitful. Summarize Luke 13:6-9 here.

What can we do to become more fruitful?

What happens to those who are unfruitful?

Consider some creative ways we can bring Christ into the world. Be prepared to discuss this question with your small group.

Write a prayer asking God to give you the wisdom and courage to pass His light on to someone who does not know the gospel.

Day Four

I Am

"'I am the Alpha and the Omega,' says the Lord God, 'who is, and who was, and who is to come, the Almighty.'" Revelation 1:8

Who are you really? We tend to change depending on the situation. We have different personas for how we need to interact with different people or how we need to react to changing circumstances. Jesus never changed. He continued to describe Himself as the Light of the World. This outraged the Pharisees. Read more about it in John 8:12-20. What is the *Light of Life*, described in this passage?

Write John 8:12 here, and consider committing this verse to memory.

It is time for a little excursion to explore this particular statement in greater detail. John 8:12 is the second of seven *I am* statements Jesus made, recorded in the gospel of John. Write the *I am* statements here.

1. John 6:35

   John 6:48

2. John 8:12

   John 9:5

3. John 10:7

4. John 10:11-14

5. John 11:25

6. John 14:6

7. John 15:1

   John 15:5

Why are these I am statements so important?

Do you recall how God identifies Himself? Turn to Exodus 3:14. Who does God say He is?

Jesus tells us who He is in John 8:58. What does Jesus say?

Throughout Jesus' ministry, He consistently tells us who He is, who sent Him, and why He is here. There is never any question about it. We also learn a great deal about Jesus, the light, from the way He helped others. According to John 9:1-12, what miracle did Jesus perform?

Jesus performed more than a miracle. He took this opportunity to teach a spiritual truth. What is it?

Jesus expands on this lesson when He learns of the death of His friend, Lazarus. John 11:4-11 tells us Jesus intentionally waits for two more days before going to Lazarus.

Meanwhile, He teaches another spiritual truth before raising Lazarus from the dead. What does Jesus mean in verse 9, "they see by this world's light," and verse 10, "for they have no light?"

Walking without God will lead us in the wrong direction. What do you do to ensure you are not headed in the wrong direction spiritually?

In John 12:35-36, Jesus tells His disciples of His imminent death. The verses are reprinted below.

> "Then Jesus told them, 'You are going to have the light just a little while longer. Walk while you have the light, before darkness overtakes you. Whoever walks in the dark does not know where they are going. Believe in the light while you have the light, so that you may become children of light.' When he had finished speaking, Jesus left and hid Himself from them." John 12:35-36.

Circle, or highlight, each phrase that discusses light. With a different color, circle, or highlight the phrases that mention darkness. What warning was Jesus giving in this passage?

What promise was He giving to us?

Jesus used light as one way to express the truth and Himself. Light is a metaphor for what is pure and true. Follow the light of Jesus and see truth revealed.

Write a prayer asking God to help you identify who you are in Him.

Day Five

The False Angel of Light

"Do not be yoked together with unbelievers. For what do righteousness and wickedness have in common? Or what fellowship can light have with darkness?" 2 Corinthians 6:14

What happens to a dark room when you turn on the light? The darkness goes away. Light makes the room a more welcoming place. It is the same with the light of Christ. We are drawn to His light because light makes the darkness go away. Children seem to understand this naturally—they want to sleep with a night light on.

To truly understand light we should have a basic understanding of darkness and what darkness represents. God is separate and distinct from darkness (1 John 1:5). Darkness and light cannot coexist. Darkness (often a metaphor for life without God) was a theme Jesus often taught about.

Look at Matthew 8:10-12. What happens to those without faith?

Yesterday, we looked at John 12:35-36, two power-packed verses. What are the two phrases that discuss darkness in these verses?

If you do not know where you are going, what are you?

What does Jesus tell us about darkness in John 12:46?

Belief in Christ will bring us light; we can leave the darkness behind. Possibly the clearest lesson on darkness is in John 3:16-21, a passage we looked at on day three. Focus on verses 19-21. Why do people love the darkness?

What happens to people who live by the truth?

How many times does the word *light* appear in these three verses?

We are called to follow the light of Christ.

Some of the great philosophical questions of the ages are, "Why is there evil (Satan)?" and "When did Satan come into existence?" Scripture provides information regarding Satan. In the book of Job we see Satan asking to test a man. What do we learn about Satan and his power from Job 1:6-12?

We do not know exactly when Satan fell but we do know he fell before he tempted Eve in the Garden of Eden. Before he fell, Satan was Lucifer (Isaiah 14:12 KJV). Satan's fall is described in Isaiah 14:12-23 and Ezekiel 28:11-19. You will want to read the text in more than one version.

What did Lucifer look like before he fell?

Where did he hang out?

What happened because of his beauty?

Where did God send him?

What will he be remembered for? (Isaiah 14:20-23, NET or HCSB Translation)

Nothing. I had not thought about it before, but when we enter God's Kingdom there will be no reason to remember the evil one. Imagine never being remembered. It will be like he never existed. This thought is confirmed in Isaiah 65:17. Write it here.

What does Revelation 21:4 tell us about the old order of things?

Does this verse give you any insight into heaven?

Foresight

Reread the creation story, this time in The Message Version. The first two verses are reprinted below.

> "First this: God created the Heavens and Earth—all you see, all you don't see.
> Earth was a soup of nothingness, a bottomless emptiness, an inky blackness.
> God's Spirit brooded like a bird above the watery abyss.
> God spoke: "Light!"
> And light appeared.
> God saw the light was good and separated light from dark.
> God named the light Day, he named the dark Night.
> It was evening, it was morning—Day One." Genesis 1:1-2 (MSG)

Use a dictionary to look up the word *brooded* (second line) in a dictionary. What does brooded mean in this context?

What does this definition tell you about what God knew, or what precautions He took to protect His creation?

Write a prayer asking God to protect you and help you recognize darkness, and give you wisdom and courage to flee from it (1 Corinthians 10:13).

"Thus the heavens and the earth were completed in all their vast array." Genesis 2:1

WEEK THREE

The Heavens

Day One

The Sun, Moon, and Stars

*"He changes times and seasons; He deposes kings
and raises up others. He gives wisdom to the wise
and knowledge to the discerning." Daniel 2:21*

The glare of city lights dulls the grandeur of the night sky. Take an imaginary trip away from the city and envision the darkness poked full of sparkling lights. Consider the constellations that move with the seasons. Ponder the phases of the moon and the traveling planets. Contemplate the rhythm of day and night. Perhaps the night sky is more than a pretty night light. Maybe the stars hold a message.

On the fourth day of creation we see God creating the light we can see. Read Genesis 1:14-19. Note everything God made on the fourth day of creation, and the reasons He created these objects.

What do you notice about the fourth day of creation?

On the fourth day, God concentrated on the sun, moon, and stars. He had specific reasons for doing so. We understand the sun and the moon are two great lights. Verse 14b tells us, "and to serve as signs to mark sacred times, and days and years."

God provided us a way to understand and track the passage of time. Do you think this is important? Why or why not?

The Jewish Calendar

The moon was important to the Israelites. In ancient times, a new month began with a new moon. A cycle of the moon is about 29 ½ days. A lunar year, or twelve lunar cycles total 354 days, or eleven days less than the solar year, which is 365 ¼ days (our modern calendar is based on the solar year). The Jewish calendar adds a month every few years to make up for the difference and to ensure the festivals occur during the correct seasons.[24]

God commanded several festivals each year. What festivals did the Lord require in Exodus 23:14-16, and why?

Festivals are also discussed later in Scripture. What festivals are mentioned in 2 Chronicles 8:12-13?

The night sky was the Israelites calendar. Return to Genesis 1:14. This verse uses the words *sacred times*. What do these sacred times mean to you?

We still celebrate an important sacred time that is based on the lunar calendar. Easter is set each year as the first Sunday on or after the first full moon, after the first day of Spring. This date also affects the dates for Ash Wednesday, Palm Sunday, Good Friday, and Pentecost.

The Jewish day is also different than our secular day. The Jews based the day on the creation story—evening and morning. The Jewish day began at sundown, but it was still a twenty-four hour period of time. It was a routine for the Jews, just as our day is routine for us. Day, night, the phases of the moon, and the seasons provide us a certain predictability and routine to life. Do you see predictability as a gift from God? Why or why not?

What do the following verses tell us about the predictability of the calendar?

Genesis 8:22

Psalm 104:19

Predictability is a gift from God. The seasons and calendar repeat, sowing and harvesting are methodical and deliberate. Holidays are anticipated. We need moments to worship, to work, and to rest. We know the morning will come again, and the Spring will return. Similarly, we can count on God day in and day out. The Lord's goodness and love for us is predictable.

Different Roles

God made each part of His creation in a unique manner. Explain what the phrase, *differences in splendor,* means in 1 Corinthians 15:41.

Different does not mean good or bad, better than or less than. Different simply means *not the same*. Each star has a different purpose; each of us is here for a different purpose too. We all play an important role in the body of Christ, and we are all to work together for the glory of God (1 Corinthians 12:15-20).

Write a prayer thanking God for the seasons, festivals,
and sacred times to worship Him.

Day Two

Promises in the Stars

"David did not take the number of the men twenty years old or less, because the Lord had promised to make Israel as numerous as the stars in the sky." 1 Chronicles 27:23

Children love field trips. One of my favorites was going to the planetarium. In the middle of the day the lights went out, and we could see a representation of the night sky. The speaker would describe the horizon, planets, stars, constellations, and galaxies. My favorite program included the stories the ancients made up about the constellations. The stars seemed to come to life on that field trip. What treasures are hidden in the stars?

Return to Genesis 1:16. Notice the complete sentence in the verse, "He also made the stars." We know every bit of Scripture is important, what is so important about this particular sentence?

Stars are used as metaphors of God's glory; they help us understand that God is infinite. Read Job 22:12. What do you perceive about God's location in this verse?

What does Psalm 8:3-4 tell us about creation?

What do you notice about God's capabilities in Psalm 147:4-5?

References to the stars help us understand God's infinite power, including His limitless love.

The Promise in the Metaphor

In several areas of Scripture, we see stars are used as a metaphor for a promise or a prophecy. In later passages we see the fulfillment of that prophecy. Consider Genesis 15:5. What is the promise?

What is the promise in Genesis 26:3-5?

Who was the promise made to?

How many men were in the census according to Numbers 1:46?

Multiply that number by four.

Women and children were not counted in the census. It is safe to say the promise to Abraham was fulfilled by the census in Numbers 1, and continued for centuries thereafter.

What does Deuteronomy 1:10 tell us about this promise?

The fulfillment of this promise is repeated in Hebrews 11:12. According to this verse, how many descendants came from this one man?

God kept his promise to Abraham. God still keeps His promises to us today.

Joseph's Dreams

Do you recall Joseph and his dreams? What do the stars represent in Genesis 37:9?

What do the sun and moon represent?

Generally, we understand the eleven stars represent Joseph's eleven brothers. Knowing what the sun and moon represent is not as clear. Several chapters later, after Joseph has been in slavery for a number of years, Joseph explains the pharaoh's dreams (Genesis 41:16-40). The pharaoh is so impressed that in verse 40 he states, "all my people are to submit to your orders."

The ancient Egyptians worshiped thousands of gods. Ra or Re was the god of the sun, and was the Egyptian's most important god. Every night the Egyptians thought Ra would travel across the sky in a sun boat.[25] This left the moon to light the world. The moon god was Thoth. He was an adviser of the gods, and the representative of the sun god, Ra.[26] The sun and moon in Joseph's dreams may have represented the Egyptians.

Joseph's insight from God elevated him to the second most powerful position in Egypt. His wisdom and guidance saved the Egyptians from starvation, as well as people from several other countries.

Does God still speak to us in dreams?

What other ways does God speak to us today?

Write a prayer thanking God for keeping His promises to us.

Day Three

Direction

*"He is the Maker of the Bear and Orion, the Pleiades
and the constellations of the south." Job 9:9*

We are surprised at the mysterious lives of nocturnal animals. Perhaps we are just as much an oddity to them. They are God's creatures too, and they seem to be doing quite well at night. That is because even on nights with no moon there is some light. Return to the fourth day of creation and study Genesis 1:16. What *lights* does this verse focus on?

The phrase, two great lights, refers to the sun and moon. While the sun and moon may govern the day and night, they do not diminish the purpose of the stars. Stars were important to the ancients for navigation. Sailors used constellations to help find their way. The Bible tells us constellations were recognized early in world history (Job 9:9).

The North Star

The heavens are more than a beautiful sight. God gave us tools in the night sky to act as a guide to help us find our way home. He made it easy by placing the North Star, or Polaris, over the north axis of the earth. The North Star does not appear to move. Using the North Star as a guide, you can determine south, west, and east, and find your way.[27] God did not forget our southern neighbors. They do not have a *South Star*. Instead, they have the Southern Cross, a constellation that points to what should be a South Star.[28]

Do you think the North Star, Southern Cross, and other constellations are relevant or random? Why?

Reread Genesis 1:14-19, the account of the fourth day of creation. Note every word or phrase that pertains to the stars God created.

What did God create the stars for?

Verse 14 notes the stars are to serve as signs. Stars can also serve as tools. A compass works by pointing its needle north, to the North Pole. Once you know north, you can find the rest of the directions.[29] Name the tools used in Psalm 43:3-4. (You may need to read these verses in more than one version.)

Why does the Psalmist need these tools?

My husband is an avid mountain biker. He bikes on clearly marked trails, but he also uses a GPS, our modern compass. He wants a guide, a sure way to find his way home. Gerry does not rely on his senses, he trusts the guide, the compass. God can be our compass, if we let Him. He tells us so in Proverbs 3:5-6. Record the verses here and consider committing them to memory.

What does the phrase, *make your paths straight*, mean to you?

What did we learn about how light travels during week one, day three?

Light travels in a straight line, the most direct way possible.[30] God has a specific plan for us; He gives us a direct path to that goal. Anytime we detour it is because the detour was our own choice. We have to learn to lean on God who knows the true direction for our lives.

Note a time when you went off the course God planned for your life. How did you get back on course?

I am relieved I do not have to figure out everything on my own. If I ask, God will keep me on the course He has planned for me. He is willing to do the same for each one of us.

Write a prayer asking God to help you follow His guidance
and direction for your life.

Day Four

The Magi's Story

"After Jesus was born in Bethlehem in Judea, during the time of King Herod, Magi from the east came to Jerusalem." Matthew 2:1

There are only a few *big* moments in our lives such as baptism, graduation, marriage, and the birth of our children. We may consider some of these *sacred* events. God refers to sacred times during the creation story. Refer to the fourth day of creation when God made the sun, moon, and stars. Consider Genesis 1:14 again. What are some sacred events in your life, and in world history?

What could be more sacred than marking the birth of Christ?

What you think the star of Bethlehem looked like as it hung over the stable where Jesus was born? Describe it, or draw it here.

The birth of Christ was a holy event, announced by God, in God's way. Hollywood, music, and Christmas pageants have conditioned us to imagine the night of Christ's birth was a spectacular theatrical production. Nativity scenes have caused us to believe the star that led the Magi was a brilliant star. What in all of Scripture would lead us to that conclusion? Angels and shepherds were all the fanfare our King of Kings received that first Christmas night. A brilliant star would have attracted hundreds, if not thousands of people to come investigate, and that would have been well documented. Maybe the star that led the Magi was something different.

Two gospels provide information on the birth of Christ. The gospel of Luke focuses on the actual birth and shepherds. The gospel of Matthew is the only gospel to mention a star. Read Matthew 2:1-12, then note every phrase containing the word *star*.

What do you notice concerning the star in this passage?

The text explains the wise men saw the star of Bethlehem, and set out on their journey. How long did the trip take? A journey from the east must have taken at least a few months. Once they arrived, the Magi did not find the baby King where they expected to find Him. Imagine what the Magi must have thought. Were they wrong? Was their long journey for nothing? Suppose the star was not visible the entire time the wise men were on their journey. Consider the Message Version of the narrative.

> "Instructed by the king, they set off. Then the star appeared again, the same star they had seen in the eastern skies. It led them on until it hovered over the place of the child. They could hardly contain themselves: There were in the right place! They had arrived at the right time!" Matthew 2:9-10 (MSG)

Circle, or highlight, what the star did.

We can see from Scripture that when the Magi saw the star *again* they were overjoyed. The text indicates the star must have disappeared for a time. Does this mean the star appeared only on the night of Christ's birth, then again to lead the wise men? We cannot be certain. Consider this; if the star was visible for the entire length of the journey, others may have investigated the astronomical phenomena. There would be secular documentation of the star. Why were there no others to follow or at least investigate? Was this a star, or something else? Was the star of Bethlehem the Holy Spirit?

What sign are the shepherds told to look for in Luke 2:8-12?

Hum. The shepherds are not told to look for a star. They are told to look for a baby lying in an animal's feeding trough. The shepherds were terrified by the presence of the heavenly host, but not for long. They quickly left their flocks and went to find the baby Jesus, just as they were told. Luke's narrative mentions several other details, why omit something as significant as a star?

Our Lord came to earth in the most humble way possible. The star of Bethlehem may have been a small, humble star, a star God would have chosen. That would mean the star was not the glorious star we are conditioned to believe it was. Perhaps the star of Bethlehem was an announcement for a chosen few.

Write a prayer thanking God for the sacred moments in our lives and the sacred birth of our Lord and Savior, Jesus Christ.

Day Five

Witness Protection Program

"Our God is a God who saves; from the
Sovereign Lord comes escape from death." Psalm 68:20

How many times have we looked at a particular thing and not noticed the details? We become so accustomed to our environment that we do not realize objects, or words are there (or not there). We make assumptions. The same holds true with certain stories from the Bible. What truths are we missing as a result of rushing through Scripture? Consider the timing of the visit of the Magi in Matthew 2:13-15. What is Joseph told to do in his dream?

Escape. It is a key word. *Escape* implies there is danger involved. You leave quickly, and you take very little with you.

When did they leave?

Imagine if you had to flee your home in the middle of the night. What would you be able to take with you? Starting a new life in another country is expensive no matter what century you lived in. Maybe God sent the wise men with gifts to fund the escape to Egypt at precisely the time those funds were needed. Review Matthew 2:9-10. The Message Version is reprinted below.

> "Instructed by the king, they set off. Then the star appeared again, the same star they had seen in the eastern skies. It led them on until it hovered over the place of the child. They could hardly contain themselves: They were in the right place! They had arrived at the right time!" Matthew 2:9-10

Highlight the last sentence. The Magi had arrived at the right time. We can all think of times when we found the perfect parking place, or did not have to wait in line, but substantially speaking, how often has God been right on time for you? Note a personal experience where, looking back, you know God's timing was right in your life.

Not only is God's timing perfect, His entire plan is flawless. Take a look at time past, before creation, and see where God planned our salvation. Record Ephesians 1:4 here and consider committing it to memory.

If God planned our salvation, before creation, Christ must have been present at creation. The following verses support the fact Jesus was present when the world was made. Paraphrase them.

John 17:24

1 Peter 1:20

Write the last sentence of 2 Timothy 1:9 here.

Did God put the star of Bethlehem in the heavens at the time of creation? Notice the word *before* in the previous three verses. Further evidence God's plan is also written in the heavens is provided in additional verses throughout Scripture. Paraphrase the following verses here.

Psalm 8:3

Psalm 147:4

Job 22:12

1 Corinthians 15:41

Notice that God even loves the stars enough to name them. These Scriptures, and the account of creation, indicate the richness and vastness of God's great design. God planned to love you before creation. He loved you so much God had a plan of redemption when He crafted the universe. According to Revelation 13:8, when was the Lamb slain?

What an immeasurable act of love! When you realize God planned our salvation, before creation, what should we do?

Write a thank you note to God for His plan of redemption,
prepared before creation.

"Your thunder was heard in the whirlwind, Your lightning lit up the world; the earth trembled and quaked." Psalm 77:18

WEEK FOUR

Gifts from Heaven

Day One	Sunrise, Sunset
Day Two	Rain
Day Three	Thunder
Day Four	Lightning
Day Five	Clouds

Day One

Sunrise, Sunset

"His splendor was like the sunrise; rays flashed from His hand, where His power was hidden." Habakkuk 3:4

Some of the prettiest sights in nature are sunrises and sunsets. High, light clouds, fair winds, and the rising or setting sun come together to create a masterpiece on the horizon. From grade-school science, we know the earth rotates once every twenty-four hours, creating our day and night cycles. Therefore, we could enjoy a sunrise and sunset every day (weather permitting). Should we stop to enjoy such beauty? Why or why not?

When we notice the sun, let us be reminded to praise the Lord. What does Ecclesiastes 11:7 tell us about the light and sun?

Who is mentioned in each of these verses that describe the sunrise: 2 Samuel 23:4; Habakkuk 3:4, and Hosea 6:3?

Record Psalm 113:3 here and consider committing this verse to memory.

Enjoying God's creation is an opportunity for praise and worship. God intended for us to enjoy His creation, including the sunrise and sunset. In ancient times the sunrise and sunset were also used as measurement tools. What is measured in Numbers 34:15, Deuteronomy 11:30, and Psalm 113:3?

What is measured in Deuteronomy 24:15?

Measurement also helps us understand the concept of boundaries, crucial for functioning appropriately within a society. Like a good parent, God gives us boundaries to keep us safe and healthy, as well as an understanding of who God is and what He is capable of. What boundaries are you thankful for?

What new boundaries do you need to set in your life?

The Sun Stands Still

I live in Texas. On a hot summer day, the sun seems to be standing still. Thousands of years ago there was a day when the sun did stand still. Peruse Joshua 10:12-15. What was Joshua's request?

Why did Joshua make this request?

Describe Joshua's faith.

What was the outcome?

Bookstore shelves are lined with devotionals, replete with stories telling us of God working in the lives of today's saints, in wondrous ways. While we find it uplifting to hear another person's story, your story also has power. What is your story of faith?

How comfortable are you sharing your faith story, or personal testimony?

If you have not been comfortable discussing your faith with others, pray about sharing your story with someone this week, in a safe environment. Faith shared is powerful.

Write a prayer thanking God for the opportunity to enjoy
His precious creation. Ask Him for the courage
to express your faith in Him.

Day Two

Rain

"He provides rain for the earth; He sends
water on the countryside." Job 5:10

Rain is a welcome gift during Texas summers. Anytime a storm is over I look for a rainbow. The lighting is not always quite right, but when the rainbow does appear, it is a spectacular phenomenon. The rainbow is the water in the atmosphere refracting the sunlight, like millions of tiny prisms.[31] Today we will explore this extraordinary gift from God. Study Genesis 9:12-17.

A covenant is a formal agreement to do something specific. How many times is the word *covenant* used in this story?

How many times is the word *rainbow* used?

God used the word *covenant* twice as often as He used the word *rainbow*. Was this because God was more interested His promise, the covenant, than the symbol? Put a bookmark on that thought for a moment.

Our miraculous little planet is covered by approximately 70 percent water. Due to weather patterns, there are thousands of showers or storms around the globe every day.[32] The sun is constantly shining through the earth's atmosphere; therefore, God's rainbow is a permanent fixture somewhere in the earth's sky. Both water and light are required for rainbows to appear.[33] When the rainbow appears, we remember God promised not to destroy the earth by flood ever again (Genesis 9:9-16). However, the rainbow is more. God is sending His *light* to us through the water, creating a rainbow, a constant reminder of His light, His love, and His *covenant*.

Would it surprise you that the word *rainbow* is used in other places in Scripture? There are three references to rainbows outside of the Noah story: Ezekiel 1:28, Revelation 4:1-6, and Revelation 10:1. Summarize these verses here.

Imagine the grandeur of these holy scenes. The rainbow, a reminder of God's covenant, surrounds Him.

To Evoke Pharaoh's Attention

A tornado hit the apartment building my husband and I lived in when we were first married. The rain and wind were very strong and we heard the sound of wood breaking. Suddenly, rain started pouring in our apartment, but God kept us safe. Severe weather can be frightening, but it can also be a gift from God. Read Exodus 9:17-26 and note verse 26 here.

God was specific about where He sent the hail. What does this tell you about God's protection?

Describe a time when God protected you, and pause to thank Him for caring for you.

Manna and Quail

Another gift from the heavens came while the Israelites were in the desert. Use Exodus 12:37 to estimate the number of people who fled Egypt.

A safe estimate is two million people, but the population could have been as high as three million. During this time the Israelites were basically nomads. The desert could not have supported the population for more than a few months, let alone forty years. What did the Lord say to Moses in Exodus 16:4-33?

When were the people to gather the manna?

Were there other miracles in the manna? What were they?

The miracle of manna was indeed food, but consider how nutritionally balanced the Israelites diet was. There is no record of vegetable gardens in the desert. We don't read about a variety of fruit trees. The manna and quail contained all the nutrition the Israelites needed to properly sustain life—for four decades! (I would like some of those vitamins.) List some of the ways the Lord generously provides for you.

Write a prayer thanking God for always providing for you,
including the ways you do not see.

Day Three

Thunder

*"The Lord thundered from heaven; the voice of
the Most High resounded." 2 Samuel 22:14*

The power displayed in a thunderstorm is both miraculous and terrifying. We watch
the sky provide a dazzling light show while we listen to the symphony of thunder. You
can smell the rain and feel its refreshment. At the same time you sense the electricity
in the air. Nature is both delightful and terrifying. When God shows up we often see
the same power, and light is usually involved. Several such instances occur throughout
the Bible. Scripture documents unusual occurrences, unique gifts from heaven, God's
power demonstrated for a specific purpose, and glimpses of heaven.

The Ten Commandments

Moses spent time on Mount Sinai, the mountain of God, and in the presence of God.
There he received the Ten Commandments. How did God sound and appear to the
people in Exodus 20:18-19?

The prophet Jeremiah describes God's power manifested in nature. Read Jeremiah
51:15-16. Should we have a fear of nature? Why or why not?

What is the difference between fear and respect?

Should we have a fear of God? Explain.

Jesus was not afraid of the storm when He walked on the water (Matthew 14:22-33, Mark 6:45-52 and John 6:16-21). How should we properly respond to the forces of nature?

The Baptism of Jesus

Three synoptic gospel writers remarked on the baptism of Jesus. The event must have been very important. Even Christ's birth is not described in all the gospels. Read Matthew 3:16, Mark 1:10, and Luke 3:21. What do you notice from these three accounts of Jesus' baptism?

Heaven was opened and the Holy Spirit descended on Christ. Here, we see all three persons of the Trinity during the baptism of Jesus.[34] Jesus' baptism was also the commissioning of His entrance into the ministry. Jesus refers to heaven opening in John 1:51. "He then added, 'Very truly I tell you, you will see heaven open, and the angels of God ascending and descending on the Son of Man.'" What do you think it means to *open heaven*?

In Genesis 28:10-22, Jacob dreamed about a ladder from heaven, in which the angels were ascending and descending. God spoke to Jacob in this dream, giving a promise to Jacob and his descendants. The disciples would have known this story from the Torah and understood Christ's claim and God's promise to be with His people.

The Temple Veil

We saw God open heaven for His Son to start His ministry. What does God do at the end of Jesus' earthly life? Review the accounts of the moment of Jesus' death; Matthew 27:51-53, Mark 15:37-39, and Luke 23:44-46. What identical thing happened in each passage?

The temple veil was a thick curtain, sixty-feet long, thirty-feet wide, and four-inches thick. Three hundred priests were needed to hang it.[35] The temple veil separated the presence of God from His people. At the moment of Christ's death the veil was torn from top to bottom. Now, people had free access to God. Consider how difficult it would be to rip this thick veil. God uses His power to reveal Himself in ways that only God can.

Write a prayer recommitting yourself to discovering
the power of God in your life, and fulfilling the purposes
God created you for.

Day Four

Lightning

*"Do you know how God controls the clouds and
makes His lightning flash:" Job 37:15*

A bolt of lightning will change the appearance of the sky for a few seconds. A number
of atmospheric phenomena must be going on simultaneously for lightning to strike.
We do not know where or when lightning will strike, it is a fleeting thing. The change
God provides, however, is permanent. The gift of Christ to our world represented
enormous change, primarily in our relationship with God; but also how to view the
law and the prophets that represented centuries of tradition to the Jewish people.

The Transfiguration

Use both a dictionary and a thesaurus to define the word *transfiguration.*

Read the accounts of the transfiguration (Matthew 17:1-3, Mark 9:2-4, and Luke
9:28-30). What details do you glean from these passages?

Jesus was glorified during the transfiguration. His appearance was like lightning. Who
else appeared transfigured?

Two millennia before cameras, how do you think the disciples knew who the other two transfigured images were?

The disciples were given the opportunity to behold Christ as deity. Do you think this affected the disciple's understanding of who Christ was? Why or why not?

Do you think we will appear transfigured when we get to heaven? Why or why not?

The Second Coming of Christ

Heaven is our real home. One day, Jesus will return for His people. Read about this momentous event in Matthew 24:30-31, and Luke 17:24, then note what His return will be like. (Look at the verses in more than one version.)

Jesus uses the same metaphor in both passages. What is it?

Is this significant? Why?

We know Jesus will take us to heaven because of several passages in Scripture. Read and paraphrase each.

Daniel 7:13-14

John 14:1-4

Hebrews 9:28

1 Thessalonians 4:16-17

The Tomb Opens

All three of the synoptic gospels discuss the most important event in all history—the empty tomb. Describe what happened in Matthew 28:1-10, Mark 16:1-7, and Luke 24:1-8.

Describe the appearance of the angels who delivered the message to the women who visited the tomb.

Do you think there is significance to the color of the angel's attire? Why?

The description of *lightning* may have been the gospel writers only form of reference to describe this remarkable color. Today we could probably add more adjectives, but it would still be an attempt to describe the color. I suspect the white of the transfiguration and the white the angels wore is a color that will not be seen again, until we arrive in heaven.

Write a prayer asking God to give you the ability to recognize His power when it is displayed.

Clouds

"At that time people will see the Son of Man coming in
clouds with great power and glory." Mark 13:26

My daughter recently reminded me of the fun childhood pastime of looking at clouds and pretending they are in the shapes of animals. I giggled with her as she pointed to a puppy, a bunny, and a dragon. What a great day it will be when we will no longer imagine, but see Christ coming for us in the clouds (Matthew 24:30-31)!

The Ascension of Christ

The last earthly act of Christ was to give the Great Commission. It is found in two gospels, Matthew 28:18-20, and Mark 16:15-16. Write one of them here.

Immediately after Jesus delivered the Great Commission, He ascended into heaven (Mark 16:19). What is the significance of Jesus giving the church its mission just before He ascended?

During my years in the United States Navy, I witnessed several change of command ceremonies. Many of these ceremonies included the retirement of the departing officer, usually after the officer reached the pinnacle of his or her career. The significant part of the ceremony was passing the command of the ship or base from one leader to another leader. This signified the command structure and mission would continue, no matter who was in charge.

Do you think the ascension of Christ signified Christ's earthly mission was accomplished and there was a change of command for the church? Why or why not?

On the morning of His resurrection Jesus spoke about His upcoming ascension. Study John 20:16-18, paying particular attention to verse 17. Where does Jesus say He is going?

Why do you think the concept of *ascension* was not fully developed prior to Jesus' actual ascension?

The apostle Paul explains the importance of the ascension in Ephesians 4:7-13. What does Christ's ascension mean in this passage?

An explanation of verse 9 may be found in the Apostle's Creed. (When reciting the creed, some people omit line 8.)

The Apostle's Creed

1. I believe in God, the Father Almighty,
2. the Maker of heaven and earth,
3. and in Jesus Christ, His only Son, our Lord:

4. Who was conceived by the Holy Ghost,
5. born of the Virgin Mary,
6. suffered under Pontius Pilate,
7. was crucified, dead and buried;
8. He descended into hell.
9. The third day He rose again from the dead;
10. He ascended into heaven,
11. and sitteth at the right hand of God the Father Almighty;
12. from thence he shall come to judge the quick and the dead.
13. I believe in the Holy Ghost;
14. the holy catholic church;
15. the communion of saints;
16. the forgiveness of sins;
17. the resurrection of the body;
18. and the life everlasting.   Amen.

The author of Hebrews explains the ascension concept further. What does Hebrews 4:14-16 tell us about who Jesus is and what He understands?

Jesus lived as a human. He experienced tremendous rejection, pain, and suffering. He identifies with your sorrows and your needs.

*Write a prayer thanking Christ for understanding you
and interceding for you. Commit to do your part in fulfilling
the Great Commission.*

*"I looked, and I saw a windstorm coming out of the north—
an immense cloud with flashing lightning and
surrounded by brilliant light." Ezekiel 1:4*

WEEK FIVE

Light Shows

Day One

Fireworks

"Why, you do not even know what will happen tomorrow. What is your life? You are a mist that appears for a little while and then vanishes." James 4:14

Tradition tells us the earliest forms of firecrackers were created in China.[36] Various chemicals are added to the gunpowder to create the colors we see during the spectacular displays.[37] These colorful explosions cannot compare to the sight of burning sulfur that rained down on Sodom, Gomorrah, and the surrounding plain (Genesis 19:24). When sulfur burns, it emits a blue flame.[38] Blue fire rained down from the sky and the area was destroyed.

There is more to the story of Sodom and Gomorrah. Peruse Genesis 18:16-33. Why did Abraham plead for Sodom?

What was the final number of people that had to be righteous for God to spare Sodom?

The narrative continues in chapter 19. According to verses 15-29, who was spared from the destruction of Sodom and Gomorrah?

Why was this family spared?

What does this small number of survivors tell you about sharing the gospel of Christ today?

What specific instructions were given to Lot's family as they fled Sodom?

Why was Lot's family not allowed to look back at the devastation?

What does this story tell you about obedience?

What do you learn about remaining pure from this story?

Wheel in the Sky

Another unusual sight in the heavens is described in Ezekiel 1. The prophet Ezekiel was also a priest. He was among the Jews taken captive and exiled to Babylon in 597 B.C.[39]

Ezekiel was provided a unique vision of the sky. Ezekiel described what he saw with the forms of reference available to him at that point in history. Translating the text from one language to another is not precise either. It is difficult for any scholar to be sure exactly what each portion of Ezekiel's vision represents. What do you think Ezekiel saw in chapter 1? (It may be helpful to read the text in more than one version.)

What references to light are listed in the passage, and what do they describe?

Verse 4

Verse 13

Verse 14

Verse 27

Verse 28

Ezekiel's references to light are ultimately a description of the glory of God. Imagine being given that same vision. How would you describe God?

Write a prayer asking God to keep your heart pure
and thank Him for the opportunity to approach
the throne of grace.

Day Two

The Creative Earth

"The heavens declare the glory of God; the skies
proclaim the work of His hands." Psalm 19:1

Our planet creates light. The earth's magnetic poles and radiation from the sun team up to create the phenomena known as the Aurora Borealis, or the Northern Lights. (There are also Southern Lights, called the Aurora Australis.) Charged particles from the sun, called the solar wind, move along the earth's magnetic fields toward the north and south poles. There the solar wind collides with particles in the earth's atmosphere. Many of these particles release an electron and create tremendous light shows.[40] These displays are more proof of God's creativity and master plan.

What do the following verses tell you about God's plan for the earth?

Genesis 8:22

Psalm 104:14-21

Isaiah 11:6-9

Isaiah 65:17-19

A Taste of Heaven

We cannot comprehend the totality of God's plan. However, creation gives us a taste of what we have to look forward to. Do you have a favorite place in nature, such as a park, a mountain, or a beach, someplace to go to be alone with God? He has prepared many delightful places for us. A small park not far from my home has a shaded pond where ducks, turtles and other animals fill the shores. I like to spend quiet, reflective time there. Sometimes I will take bread for the ducks, but usually I will stroll along the path and enjoy the beauty of the park. During my walk I feel closer to my Lord. Afterward, my spirit is remarkably refreshed and peaceful. Do you have such a place to go to recharge your spirit? Describe your retreat here.

Jesus had His special place to go. According to Luke 21:37-38 and John 8:1, where did Jesus go to be alone?

The Mount of Olives is outside Jerusalem. If you are standing on the mountain, you can see the city of Jerusalem. According to Luke 22:39, when did Jesus go there?

We do not know how often *as usual* was, but we can learn a great deal about a person from studying their habits. It was Jesus' habit to go to a place in nature to be alone. What was Jesus doing in each of these verses while He was alone?

Mark 1:35

Mark 6:46

Luke 5:16

Luke 6:12

We have a relationship with someone by spending time with them. Prayer is a relationship with God. How often do you meet with your Heavenly Father to spend time with Him for prayer, and to refresh your spirit?

Are these intervals frequent enough? Why or why not?

One answer can be found in 1 Thessalonians 5:17. Record it here.

Write a prayer thanking God for the beauty
He put into the world. Thank Him for your favorite place
in nature. Make it a point to go visit God there, soon.

Day Three

In the Furnace

*"He said, 'Look! I see four men walking around
in the fire, unbound and unharmed, and the fourth
looks like a son of the gods.'" Daniel 3:25*

The persecution of Christians has been going on since Christ was crucified. Being persecuted for worshipping the one true God goes back even further. The third chapter of Daniel tells us about three Hebrews who were literally thrown into the fire for their faith. Read the narrative and answer the following questions.

What did King Nebuchadnezzar have made?

What were its dimensions? (Use footnotes to translate to modern measurements.)

What was the King's order?

What was the punishment for refusing this order?

What did Shadrach, Meshach, and Abednego refuse to do?

That was the easy, predictable answer. Look at verse 15. Do you see the taunt? What does King Nebuchadnezzar say?

Today, are we teased and taunted because of our faith? Recall a time when you did not stand up for Christ. What were the circumstances?

How could you have responded?

Are we willing to jump into the fire for Jesus? It does not matter where we are serving, we must stand more firmly and more boldly than ever before to protect the name of Christ. We must stand up for our faith and the rights we have to pass our faith on to others, and to future generations. Discuss this topic with your small group.

What modern day images have replaced the image of King Nebuchadnezzar?

Do you *worship* any of these modern day idols in some way?

Would it be easy to stop being exposed to any of these images? How would you do it?

Considering the abundance of idols in today's culture, how easy is it for someone to follow false doctrines?

How do you stay true to the Lord's teaching?

Visualize a large furnace, large enough for men to walk around in. Imagine the furnace fully functioning, with the roar of bright orange flames dancing wildly, and casting searing heat out for several feet. What a sight it must have been to see our heroes walking around within those flames. Imagine the surprise to see a fourth man walking with them. This light show was enough to change hearts (Daniel 3:28-29).

Note a time you felt thrown into a metaphorical fire. What happened?

What did God do for you?

How can you use that story to glorify God?

Maybe you are in that fire now. Remember our Lord will be with you in the fire and see you through it.

Write a prayer thanking God for the example of strong and courageous people in the Bible.

Fire

"He makes winds His messenger, flames of
fire His servants." Psalm 104:4

I grew up in Colorado, near the mountains. I camped many times with my family, friends, and youth group. Before we pitched the tent we usually built a campfire. It was the focal point of the campsite. Many activities were around or near the campfire. We cooked over the campfire, our heat and light came from the fire, and we would sing and tell stories by the fire. The Bible uses the word and image of fire in numerous ways. God appears as fire in several areas of Scripture. Take a look at Exodus 3:1-6. How did God present Himself to Moses?

What happened to this fire?

In Leviticus 6:8-13, what must not happen to the fire on the altar?

How did God present Himself to the people in Leviticus 9:23-24?

The Fire Triangle

When an object is on fire, a chemical reaction is taking place. The object that catches on fire is changed forever. Fire needs three elements to exist: fuel, oxygen and heat. Your favorite firefighter may explain this as the fire triangle.[41]

THE FIRE TRIANGLE

OXYGEN

HEAT   FUEL

All three elements, oxygen, heat, and fuel must be present or the fire will go out. So it is with our passion (fire) for Christ. What elements must be present in our lives to keep the burning passion for Christ glowing and growing? Consider your relationship with God. What is your:

OXYGEN SOURCE–   FUEL SOURCE–

HEAT SOURCE–

Our Heavenly Father has provided us what we need to keep our passion for Him burning brightly. It is up to us, however, to stoke those flames. We can control each element needed to keep the fire burning.

Our spiritual oxygen source is our environment. Christians must place themselves in a nurturing environment. The oxygen available becomes more potent the more often you attend church, participate in Bible studies, and have fellowship with other believers. It is also important to keep yourself free from the pollution of this world. It is easy to watch R-rated movies, laugh at inappropriate jokes, or view inappropriate commercials on TV. We must keep the poisons away from our minds (Romans 12:2).

Our spiritual fuel source is the Word of God. This fuel comes from a consistent (daily) feeding on the Holy Scriptures and robust prayer life. This fuel supply is never ending. The more we learn about God the more we want to know Him, so the more fuel we will have available (Psalm 119:105).

Our spiritual heat source, or our spark, is the person of the Holy Spirit. The Holy Spirit has so much power. The moment you first believe the Holy Spirit comes to you. We must let the Holy Spirit lead us and become a stronger force in our lives if we are to become godly, more Christ-like Christian leaders (John 14:26).

The Birth of the Church

Fire represented important imagery for the Israelites. Centuries after Moses, John the Baptist discussed fire again, in the prophecy for Pentecost. What do Matthew 3:11 and Luke 3:16 tell us about fire?

Fire was involved in the birth of the church. Summarize Acts 2:1-4 here.

Our early church leaders had the fellowship and community that provided the spiritual oxygen they needed. Their spiritual fuel source was the deep understanding of the Torah and the Prophets. They also had spent time learning from Christ Himself. The third part of their spiritual fire triangle was the tongues of fire that came to rest on the believers at Pentecost. The Holy Spirit was the spark that ignited the fire of the church.

Pentecost occurred fifty days after the first Easter and shortly after the ascension of Jesus. I am not a patient person. The thought of waiting one day is irritating enough, but our early church founders waited almost two months from the time Christ rose until Pentecost. According to Acts 1:12-26, what were the disciples doing during this time?

The selection of Matthias is significant. We must pass the torch on to the next believer to carry on the mission of the church. Matthias was one of the many men who also followed Christ from the beginning of His ministry (Acts 1:21-22). Matthias had been tutored by our Lord. He had grown up in faith, so to speak. It was time for Matthias to take a leadership position. We must also pass the torch to succeeding generations.

How brightly is your spiritual fire burning? Are you as passionate about sharing your love of Christ as you were when you first became a Christian? If your fire is barely smoldering, what happened? It may be time to examine your spiritual life and give your fire more of what it needs to grow. Plot your spiritual fire on the graph below.

Ashes   Bonfire
|_____|
                                        Small campfire

Jesus expects us to burn with passion for Him, and He tells us so. Record Luke 24:32 here.

Paul gives us more information about our passion for Christ. Write Romans 12:11 here.

Consider again your passion for Jesus.

*Write a prayer asking God to increase your passion for Him,
as you share the glorious gospel of Christ in your corner
of the world.*

Day Five

Elijah

*"Listen to my cry, for I am in desperate need; rescue me from those
who pursue me, for they are too strong for me." Psalm 142:6*

Life seems difficult for every generation. When you do not know the future any bad news can make you feel desperate. Elijah lived during a turbulent period in Israel's history. During Elijah's ministry Ahab was King of Israel, and Jezebel was his wife. The people were worshipping idols and killing God's prophets. Israel had forgotten their Lord. Elijah wanted to remind the people of the power of the God of their ancestors.

Elijah Calls Down Fire

Review 1 Kings 18 and learn about the prophet Elijah. Verses 36-39 describe Elijah's sacrifice. What was the first thing Elijah did?

How did God respond?

What was the reason for Elijah's request?

The book of Leviticus explains the different types of sacrifices and offerings required by Old Testament law. These included sin offerings, guilt offerings, and drink offerings. The sacrifices were offered for various reasons. The burnt offering was made to atone for sin in general and to signify complete dedication and consecration to God. This offering was completely burned on the altar and none of it was eaten.[42] Elijah lived during a wicked period in Israel's history. He understood how important it was for a burnt offering to be made for the people.

Elijah Calls Down Fire Again

In 2 Kings 1-2 we meet Elijah again. He calls down fire to pronounce the Lord's judgment on Ahaziah. Describe God's power displayed in 2 Kings 1:9-13.

Describe Elijah's faith to summon this request of God.

Elijah Taken Up to Heaven

Few phenomena in nature possess the random power of thunder and lightning. We do not know what a storm will bring, or what the storm will leave behind. Sometimes storms bring great change. Sometimes they bring refreshment. Read 2 Kings 2:9-14. Elisha was Elijah's disciple. He had followed Elijah for years. At the end of Elijah's life, what was Elisha's request?

How was this request answered?

The imagery of the chariots and horsemen of Israel is significant for at least two reasons. First, chariots were the fastest means of transportation during those days.

Second, chariots were also used for war. Chariots and horses symbolized God's powerful protection of Israel. Elijah did more to protect and preserve Israel through God's power than military power could.[43]

Why do you think God honored Elisha's request?

The reason Elisha may have asked for a double portion of spirit is because a common practice was for the firstborn son to receive a double portion of the inheritance, and the right of succession.[44] Elisha's request shows the depth of the relationship between Elisha and Elijah.

We must be bold and strong for Christ and for our faith. Just as Elijah and Elisha remained firm during some of the worst times in Israel's history, we too must remain strong and outspoken for our true King. At some point in the future, when Jesus returns, He will have His glory. How outspoken should you be while working for Christ?

Write a prayer asking God to increase your faith and confidence in Him.

"But if serving the Lord seems undesirable to you, then choose for yourselves this day whom you will serve, whether the gods your ancestors served beyond the Euphrates, or the gods of the Amorites, in whose land you are living. But as for me and my household, we will serve the Lord." Joshua 24:15

WEEK SIX

Choices

Day One   Power

Day Two   Blinded by the Light

Day Three   A Fork in the Road

Day Four   Spiritual Blindness

Day Five   Artificial Light

Day One

Power

"Jesus replied, 'You are in error because you do not know the Scriptures or the power of God.'" Matthew 22:29

In our effort to be kind, sometimes we cower to various forms of earthly power, even when that power is misguided. While we must live in this world, it is not God's intention for us to remain silent and submit to the inappropriate use of power. We should be careful when we obey earthly authority. If that obedience is in conflict with God's Word we have a duty to speak out. We should also remember, God has the power to change hearts.

Before the apostle Paul met Jesus on the Damascus Road, he had enormous authority and power. His name was Saul. He asked the High Priest for written authority to take Christians prisoner. Saul may have even been a member of the Sanhedrin, the ancient Jewish court system.[45] In Acts 7:51-59, we find Saul involved in the persecution of Christians. Read it and keep a finger in this passage for a few minutes. What does Stephen call the Sanhedrin?

Stiff-necked and stubborn are synonyms. What does Proverbs 29:1 warn us about?

The Message Version states, "For people who hate discipline and get more stubborn, there'll come a day when life tumbles in and they break, but by then it'll be too late to help them." How do you feel about discipline after studying this verse?

I hope you welcome discipline in your life. The root of the word *discipline* is *disciple*. Meanings for the word *disciple* include "to teach or to train."[46] Discipline is designed to make us more godly people.

Have you ever thought your authority or position was threatened? What were the circumstances?

Have you ever threatened anyone? What did you do and why?

How do you think God views these actions?

What is the proper use of power or authority?

Titus 1:6-14 lists several examples of what a manager should and should not do. What does this passage say a manager should not be?

What should a manager be?

What should happen to those who fail to do good?

Does God provide power to His people? Paraphrase the following verses.

Acts 1:8

Acts 4:7-10

Ephesians: 3:16

2 Timothy 1:7

Now that you know God provides you with power through the Holy Spirit, will this change the direction of any projects or plans you have? If so, which ones, and why?

Return to Acts 7:51-59. Stephen could have thought he was abandoned by God while he was being stoned to death, but he did not. Describe the peace you think Stephen had during this brutal attack (verses 54-56).

Recall a difficult time in your life. Did you hold onto your faith like Stephen? Why or why not?

How could you have responded more appropriately?

Write a prayer asking God to show you where you have used your authority inappropriately and ask Him for forgiveness. Ask God to show you how to properly use the authority you are given.

Day Two

Blinded by the Light

"I will lead the blind by ways they have not known, along unfamiliar paths I will guide them; I will turn the darkness into light before them and make the rough places smooth. These are the things I will do; I will not forsake them." Isaiah 42:16

I was bullied as a child. I was terribly shy which made me an easier target. As bullies grow up they change their tactics, but their ultimate goal is to intimidate people. Eventually I grew up and learned to stand up for myself. Some of those bullies learned the errors of their ways and grew into fine women. Some did not.

Saul was a bully. First century Christians were easy targets, partially because there were very few Christians at the time. Read Acts 9:1-9. What was the purpose of Saul's trip to Damascus?

What was the light that flashed around Saul?

Have you ever heard God speaking to you? When?

How did you respond?

What was the first thing Jesus said to Saul?

Why is this significant?

Jesus called Saul by name because He wanted to get Saul's attention. Saul needed to understand this encounter was about his behavior. What happened to Saul as a result of this encounter with the Lord Jesus?

Saul was blinded. As a result of this blindness Saul immediately became dependent on others. Imagine this passionate man, in a position of authority, suddenly helpless. Verse 9 tells us Saul did not eat for three days after his encounter with Jesus. What do you think he did during this period of time?

It sounds like Saul was fasting. We will take a short detour here to examine the spiritual discipline of fasting. Jesus provides an excellent example of this discipline. The story of Jesus fasting and being tempted in the wilderness is found in Matthew 4:1-4 and Luke 4:1-4. What did Jesus say in these two passages?

What else does Jesus say about fasting? During the Sermon on the Mount, Jesus indicates fasting is something we do privately. What does Matthew 6:16-18 tell us about fasting?

Fasting was an important part of repentance to the Israelites. Daniel fasted and prayed (Daniel 9:3). Esther requests the nation fast and pray for her while she does the same (Esther 4:16). In Joel we see God requesting repentance through fasting (Joel 2:12). Fasting points us to a relationship with God. When Jesus was fasting in the wilderness His responses to Satan show us what our relationship with the Heavenly Father should be like. Jesus told Satan, "It is written: Man shall not live on bread alone, but on every word that comes from the mouth of God." Matthew 4:4.

Three gospels record another event regarding fasting. Paraphrase these similar passages: Matthew 9:14-15, Mark 2:18-22, and Luke 5:33-38.

Jesus tells us when the bridegroom (Jesus) is gone we will fast. It is a statement of fact. Jesus has given us direction to fast, because fasting is part of repentance and seeking guidance. After discovering Jerusalem destroyed, what did Nehemiah do (Nehemiah 1:1-4)?

Do you think Saul was fasting and praying during the three days he was blind? Why or why not?

Have you ever fasted to make a decision, as part of repentance, or the observance of Lent? What was the experience like?

Should fasting be a part of the important decision-making process? Why or why not?

Review Acts 9:5-9 again. There is the mighty Saul, brought to his knees. Notice that God gives Saul little additional information, only that he must go to the city and be told what he must do. Is Saul told how long he will wait?

Imagine you are there in the city, as instructed, waiting. Speculate what might have been going through Saul's mind.

Later in the chapter, we learn Saul waits three days. Turn to Jonah 1:17-2:9. Notice Jonah was in the belly of the great fish, for three days, after disobeying God. What similarities can you draw between these two events?

Is fasting something you should consider as part of your prayer life and journey with God? Why or Why not?

Write a prayer asking God for forgiveness for your failure to be obedient.

Day Three

A Fork in the Road

"The righteous choose their friends carefully, but the way
of the wicked leads them astray." Proverbs 12:26

When I was stationed in Japan, I drove the way the locals did—on the other side of the road. It was awkward at first, but after a few months of driving that way I was comfortable with it. When I returned to the states, I accidentally reverted to my Japanese driving habits and drove down the wrong side of a street not far from my home. Fortunately, I still had my Japanese driver's license in my wallet, and the police officer had served in the military. He let me off with a warning. Habits can be changed; but we have to recognize the habit and want to make the change.

Have you ever thought you were headed in the wrong direction spiritually? Was there an event that occurred? How did you put yourself back on the path to serving Jesus?

Peruse Acts 9:10-18. What does verse 18 mean?

How important is it to see someone's conversion?

Saul changed his tune quickly. What do we find Saul doing in Acts 9:19-28?

What caused Saul to change? Acts 26 gives us the answer. Now an apostle, Paul responds to King Agrippa. What does Paul say happened?

What appointment does Paul say he received in verses 17-18?

Change is usually a long-term process, though sometimes it can happen more quickly. I arrived at boot camp with seventy-nine other scared teenagers who, at 3:30 a.m. decided enlisting was not such a great idea. Eight weeks later a rag-tag bunch of self-centered drama queens emerged from an intense training cocoon as poised, respectful, and team-oriented sailors. The process was intense and fast. Is there something in your life you need to change? What is it?

What are you going to do to make the change happen?

How *real* is your conversion and faith in Christ? Can others see your faith and believe it? How do you know?

Who holds you accountable?

Who do you hold accountable?

How do you lift each other up?

(If you do not have accountability partner set a goal to find one during the next week.)

What do you think God has called you to do, but you have ignored?

In 1 Timothy 1:15-16, Paul calls himself the *worst sinner*. That *worst sinner* went on to write thirteen letters to various churches. Imagine if the apostle Paul ignored Jesus on the Damascus Road that day. Who would have written approximately half the New Testament? Obedience brings blessings to you and many other people. It is not too late to be obedient to God.

Write a prayer asking God to fully use you to glorify His Kingdom.

Day Four

Spiritual Blindness

"'What do you want me to do for you?' 'Lord,
I want to see,' he replied." Luke 18:41

Physical blindness is the inability to see. It is a physical condition. Spiritual blindness, however, is a choice. Proof of God exists everywhere. Advanced communication and missionary work has made it possible for most people to have heard the good news about Christ as our Lord and Savior. God's goodness is displayed in many ways. Still, God graciously gives us the choice to let Him into our lives, or not. We have to act.

Jesus gave sight to the blind at least three times; to two blind men in Matthew 9:27-31; to two blind men, including Bartimaeus, in Matthew 20:29-34, Mark 10:46-52, and Luke 18:35-43; and to the man born blind in John 9:1-12. This third account in John is especially relevant as we examine spiritual blindness. According to John 9:1-12, who does Jesus say He is?

What does the blind man have to do to gain his sight?

The blind man has to do something. Washing his eyes in the pool of Siloam is both an act of faith, and an act of obedience. The man did as he was told and he was rewarded with his sight.

The Pharisees investigate the healing in John 9:13-34. Why?

The Pharisees were looking for anything Jesus did contrary to their laws. Performing any work on the Sabbath was a violation of one of the many rules developed to comply with the Mosaic laws. Jesus opened the eyes of the formerly blind man. (He also opened the man's eyes spiritually.) When the Pharisees questioned him, the formerly blind man defended his newly gained sight, and Jesus. This angered the Pharisees even more. In verses 35-41 Jesus explains spiritual blindness. What question did the Pharisees ask?

Jesus told the Pharisees their guilt remained, angering them all the more.

Why would the Pharisees be so angry when a person received such a meaningful gift? It is difficult for us to comprehend this level of hatred. We celebrate healing. We are excited when we hear stories of miraculous recovery. We raise money to help offset the costs of medical treatment. Yet we must learn to be aware of our own shortcomings. How do we recognize our own spiritual blindness?

We are all on a spiritual journey to strengthen our relationship with God, to love Him more, worship Him more, and to be more like Him every day. In many ways we are all spiritually blind to some extent. Awareness that the journey is never over is critical to our continued spiritual growth. This awareness must lead us to a constant reevaluation of ourselves; sometimes that is difficult. We might not like what we see when we look in the mirror. The awareness should lead us to constant repentance. Prayer, Bible studies, daily devotionals, tithing, service, and fellowship with other believers will help us on our faith journey. Failure to participate in any of these activities is, in some way, spiritual blindness.

God's light has been offered to everyone. The sun shines on us all (Matthew 5:45). If we turn our back on God that is a choice we make. What can we do to prevent spiritual blindness? Record Romans 12:2 below and consider committing the verse to memory.

Darkness

Darkness is the absence of light, but do you truly know what true darkness is? When the Israelites were attempting to leave Egypt there were ten plagues. Review Exodus 10:21-23. What was the ninth plague?

How long did the plague last?

The plague of darkness was the ninth of ten plagues, the last plague before the death of the firstborn. Each plague became more intense. God graciously tried to change the pharaoh's heart but even true darkness would not cause pharaoh to change.

Have you ever personally gone through metaphorical darkness? What was the experience like?

What brought you back to the light? Was there a specific event that occurred?

The light of Christ is always available to us, no matter what sin we have committed. Open your heart to accept God's love and forgiveness. He will show you His path so you can walk in His light once more.

Write a prayer asking God to reveal any spiritual darkness in your life that you may be unaware of. Ask for forgiveness and repent.

Day Five

Artificial Light

*"Jesus said to them, 'Very truly I tell you, it is not Moses
who has given you the bread from heaven, but it is My Father
who gives you the true bread from heaven.'" John 6:32*

In an effort to increase our standard of living we may purchase copies and reproductions of more expensive items. You can buy a knock-off designer purse and sunglasses. Cubic zirconia replaces diamonds. There are grow-lights for plants that do not have access to the sun. Our food is filled with ingredients that are not really food. How do you know what is real and what is artificial?

Fold a blank sheet of paper in half. On one-half of the page, write *Direct Sun*. On the other side of the paper, write *Artificial Light*. Write down the words that come to mind when you think of these two concepts. What are the similarities and differences?

We know every living thing on earth is dependent on real sunlight, directly or indirectly.[47] The food chain needs the sun. Plants need the sun for photosynthesis. Insects and animals feed on plants. Larger animals eat smaller animals and insects, and so on. The water cycle needs the sun for evaporation and rain. We cannot exist without sunlight.

We cannot exist without God either. Some people have attempted to replace God with artificial means. They look for significance in their occupation, pursuit of influence, wealth, or power. Some think joy will come in certain leisure activities or from knowing specific people. Just as the incandescent bulb cannot bring what real sunlight can, there are many fruitless activities and events that do not bring real meaning to life. These activities can be viewed as artificial light. Artificial light can be compared to the idols of this world. What is an idol in today's world?

How Your Life is Affected by Artificial Light

Our culture demands a busy lifestyle and constant interaction with the electronic world. This busyness is to the point we push the important affairs to the side. If the devil cannot make you to stop believing, he will keep you too busy to share Christ. We must always take into consideration what the most important circumstances in life are.

God commands us to tithe. It is also important to provide time in service to God's Kingdom. The following exercise is a basic time management concept, but can be applied to a life of service as well. Use this chart to help you become more productive. There are 168 hours available to us each week. Break down what your week looks like, using the hours you have available after rest and your occupational requirements. Some activities keep us busy, but are not important. We do not concentrate on the affairs that are truly important. List your activities and the time devoted to each activity, and total your hours. The following example shows fifty hours of time available each week. Make a decision whether to increase or decrease the amount of time you spend in each activity.

Activity	Hours per week	Value to God's Kingdom	Decision
Watch TV, Movies, etc.	10	Low	Reduce / Eliminate
Play Video Games, Email, Facebook, etc.	7	Low	Reduce / Eliminate
Housework	5	High	Get Help
Girls Night Out	4	Low	Reduce / Eliminate
Run Errands	4	Medium	Combine Errands
Waiting at Restaurants / Take Out	3	Neutral	Reduce / Eliminate
Yard Work	3	Medium	Hire Service
Exercise	3	High	Increase
Prepare Meals	2	High	Increase
Family Dinners	2	High	Increase
Attend Practices	2	High	Increase
Attend Games or Performances	2	High	Increase
Attend Church	2	High	Increase
Help Kids With Homework	1	High	Increase
TOTAL:	50		

The example chart might be reworked as follows:

Activity	Hours per week	Value to God's Kingdom	Decision
Watch TV, Movies, etc.	5	Low	Reduced
Run Errands	4	Medium	Necessary
Housework	4	High	Got Help
Prepare Meals	3.5	High	Increased
Pray	3.5	High	Added
Family Dinners	3.5	High	Increased
Exercise	3.5	High	Increased
Yard Work	3	Medium	Necessary
Play Video Games, Email, Facebook, etc.	3	Low	Reduced
Pursue Healthy Friendships	3	Low	Changed

Activity	Hours Per Week	Value to God's Kingdom	Decision
Attend Practices	3	High	Increased
Attend Games or Performances	3	High	Increased
Help Kids With Homework	2	High	Increased
Attend Church	2	High	
Family Devotion	1.5	High	15 Minutes Day
Attend Bible Study	1.5	High	Added
Volunteer	1	High	Added
Waiting at Restaurants / Take Out	0	Neutral	Eliminated
TOTAL	50		

As you complete your chart, consider if your life is out of balance. Make conscious decisions about which activities are making a difference in your life and for the Kingdom, and which are not. What can you eliminate that is wasteful? Rework your chart until you have balanced your available time and removed distractions and time wasters. (You might want to make copies of this chart.)

Activity	Hours Per Week	Value to God's Kingdom	Decision

Notice that eliminating artificial light from your life brings you significantly more time to enjoy your family and serve the Lord.

How did you do with the exercise? What time wasters did you find?

What basically good activities did you find, but decided you could eliminate to make room for more fruitful activities?

What activities will you add to your life as a result of this exercise?

This is all easy to say; even the exercise is not too difficult. It is much harder to put into practice in our daily lives. Why?

The idols of this world allow us to exist in an environment that appears full of life, but such a life is empty, lonely, and totally unsatisfying. Some people we meet even pretend to be servants of God. How do they do it? Consider how Paul describes these people in 2 Corinthians 11:13-14. What do these people masquerade as?

We must be wise with those we encounter, and the activities we are involved in, but always offer Christ to the world.

Write a prayer asking God to highlight activities
that bring true value to you and His Kingdom.

"But you are a chosen race, a royal priesthood, a holy nation, a people for God's own possession, that you may proclaim the excellence of Him who called you out of darkness into his marvelous light." 1 Peter 2:9 WEB

WEEK SEVEN

Heaven on Earth

Day One — Lamps

Day Two — The Lampstand

Day Three — Seven Lampstands

Day Four — Sharing the Light

Day Five — Creation's Testimony

Day One

Lamps

"You, Lord, keep my lamp burning; my God
turns my darkness into light." Psalm 18:28

Obviously we need some sort of illumination at night and inside dark spaces. The lamps of ancient times were different from the lamps of today. Oil provided the fuel, and a wick was used for the flame. A person had to plan ahead to have enough oil to light their home for the night. The word *lamp* is used literally and metaphorically throughout Scripture. Record 2 Samuel 22:29 here and consider committing the verse to memory.

Note the similarities to the opening verse of this lesson and the verse you just transcribed. Throughout the Bible, we find *lamps* are a metaphor for God. The following verses are a sample of how the word *lamp* is used as a metaphor throughout Scripture. Write them here.

Proverbs 20:27

Revelation 21:23

Whose lamp is discussed in each of these verses?

The word *lamp* is also a metaphor for the House of David. What did the Lord promise to do in 2 Chronicles 21:4-7?

This promise is repeated in 1 Kings 15:4. Paraphrase the verse.

According to Proverbs 31:18, what are lamps a metaphor for?

Lamps are also a metaphor for honesty. Record Proverbs 13:9 here and consider committing this verse to memory.

In the following verses we see the lamp as a metaphor for God and His love. Paraphrase them.

Psalm 18:28

Proverbs 6:23-24

Shortly before His crucifixion, Jesus used lamps to teach a parable about being ready for His return. According to Matthew 25:1-13, what is the opportunity the virgins were allowed to participate in?

How many virgins were wise and prepared?

How many virgins were foolish and unprepared?

Jesus used a wedding party to explain that some people would be prepared for His return and some would not. When the time came, half the wedding party was prepared for the bridegroom, half were not.

In today's culture, how common is it to be unprepared for certain events or activities? What are some examples?

How do you stay prepared for opportunities to serve Jesus?

When was the last time you were not prepared to serve Jesus? What was the circumstance?

What can we do to encourage preparedness?

*Write a prayer asking God to help you be prepared
for opportunities to serve Him.*

Day Two

The Lampstand

*"He placed the lampstand in the tent of meeting opposite the
table on the south side of the Tabernacle." Exodus 40:24*

The word *lamp* is used numerous times throughout Scripture as we have just learned. The word *lampstand* is different. It is mentioned in only a few places in the Bible, usually in relation to the Temple of the Lord. The word *lampstand* is not even found in the dictionary. However, its importance in Scripture is significant. Beginning in Exodus 25, God provides specific instructions on how to make the lampstand for the Tabernacle. Study Exodus 25:31-40 to learn about the lampstand.

What was the lampstand made of?

How was the lampstand made?

How many lampstands were there?

How many lamps were on the lampstand?

What or who do you think the lampstand represented?

Why was the lampstand representative of Him?

We will get to that.

A *talent* of gold weighs approximately seventy-five pounds.[48] Highly skilled craftsmen were needed to create the lampstand according to God's directions. Different versions of Scripture use slightly different words, but can add significant meaning to the text. What do you notice from the King James Version? "And thou shalt make a candlestick of pure gold: of beaten work shall the candlestick be made: his shaft, and his branches, his bowls, his knops, and his flowers, shall be of the same." Exodus 25:31 (KJV)

The King James Version uses the word *beaten*. This is a foreshadowing Christ's crucifixion—Christ was beaten, but not broken.

Study Exodus 40:17-33. The Tabernacle was complete. The Israelites placed the articles, fashioned according to God's instructions, in the Tabernacle. The Tabernacle was the most holy place on earth. Placement of objects must be precise for certain reasons. Look at the diagram below. If you were standing in the Holy of Holies (representing God) looking at the priests, where was the lampstand placed?

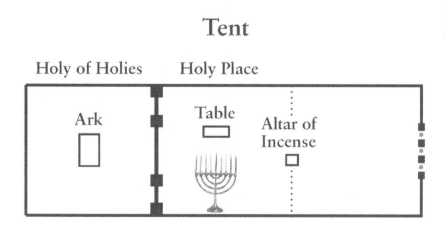

According to the following verses, where is Jesus located?

Mark 16:19

Luke 22:69

Acts 7:55

Romans 8:34

Colossians 3:1

According to these verses, Jesus is at God's right side. In the Tabernacle, we see the lampstand placed to the right of the Holy of Holies. Was the placement of the lampstand significant? Why?

The Holy of Holies represented God. The lampstand was a representation of Jesus, the Light of the World, who was to come. Jesus sits at the right hand of God, just as the lampstand was to the right of the Holy of Holies. Additionally, the light in the lampstand was never to go out. The lamp was to be kept filled with oil (Exodus 27:20-21); the lampstand was never to stop shining.

The author of Hebrews helps us to understand the Tabernacle and objects in it. Review Hebrews 9:1-10. Is it still important to study Old Testament law? Why or why not?

We cannot understand the sacrifice of Jesus without understanding the law, and reasons for the law, that came before Jesus.

History of the Lampstand

The lampstand is mentioned only a few times after the book of Numbers but they are significant stories. According to 1 Samuel 3:1-10, where was Samuel, and what objects were near him?

What were the first words God spoke to Samuel?

How does Samuel respond to God in verse 10?

This was the early anointing of Samuel, a holy event. Could God speak at an unholy place? Study Daniel 5. Where is the lampstand in this chapter?

Based on this passage, how should we treat symbols of God?

It is important to note there is a difference between a symbol of worship and worshipping a symbol. The first is used as a way to pay respect to God, the second is an idol. Is today's ceremony surrounding worship reminiscent of Temple worship? Why or why not?

Worship is orderly. In some Protestant denominations, candlesticks, representing the light of Christ, are lit at the beginning of the worship service and brought to the altar to light the altar candles. The candles remain lit the entire worship service. At the end of the worship service the flame is transferred back to the candlesticks and taken out of the sanctuary, indicating Jesus is going out into the world, and we are to follow the light of Christ.

Write a prayer asking God to shine His light so brightly in your life that you may shine His light for others.

Day Three

Seven Lampstands

"And without faith it is impossible to please God, because
anyone who comes to him must believe that he exists and that
he rewards those who earnestly seek him." Hebrews 11:6

The next reference to lampstands is found in Revelation. I struggle with understanding biblical prophecy, but after studying for this lesson I am convinced we should study prophecy more often. First, I want to know God better. If we do not study all the Scriptures, we are limiting our knowledge of our Creator. Second, God has a plan of redemption. We can have a better understanding of our place in that process by studying the prophetic books. If we study the redemptive process we can be a light in this dark world.

The Seven Churches in Asia

We put candles on birthday cakes to represent the years we have been alive, and we have stars on our flag to represent each of the states. According to Revelation 1:19-20, what do these seven lampstands represent?

In Revelation 2-3 our Lord gave a specific message to each of these churches. On the chart below, each church is listed and the Scripture reference relevant to that church. Note the warning Christ gave each church and paraphrase the reward that is possible. You may want to look at these passages in more than one version. Keep in mind these churches do not exist anymore. However, they do represent the types of churches that will exist throughout the church age.[49]

Name of Church and Scripture Reference	Warning	Reward
Ephesus Revelation 2:1-7		
Smyrna Revelation 2:8-11		
Pergamum Revelation 2:12-17		
Thyatira Revelation 2:18-29		
Sardis Revelation 3:1-6		
Philadelphia Revelation 3:7-13		
Laodicea Revelation 3:14-21		

Based on Revelation 2-3, what characteristics do you think today's church should be praised for?

What flaws should the church be warned about?

What blessings or rewards may we be missing out on due to our apathy or disobedience?

What can you do in your church to encourage obedience?

Write a prayer asking God to point out any apathy or disobedience in your life.

Day Four

Sharing the Light

"But you are a chosen people, a royal priesthood, a holy nation,
God's special possession, that you may declare the praises of him
who called you out of darkness into his wonderful light." 1 Peter 2:9

Testimony

We have all watched courtroom drama shows. Testimony is crucial to the outcome of a case. Witnesses are relied upon. On TV, the truth usually prevails, the bad guy goes to jail, and justice is served. Everyday life is rarely so black and white, but the truth is still the goal. John the Baptist testified about Jesus. Later, Jesus honors John with His words. According to John 5:31-35, how did Jesus describe John's testimony?

How else did Jesus describe John the Baptist?

Jesus is God's son, but on earth He was also fully human. He did not share His message alone. Christ delegated responsibility and authority. He sent His disciples out to share in His ministry. According to Mark 6:6-13, how were the disciples sent out?

Jesus did not intend for us to evangelize the world alone. We are to rely on each other. We help each other do God's work. How many disciples were sent out in Luke 10:1?

There were more followers of Christ than the twelve disciples. How were these additional followers sent out in this verse?

Speculate why Jesus did not send the disciples out alone.

There is safety in numbers. However, the primary reason the disciples may have traveled in pairs is they were traveling with a witness. The witness ensures the truth is revealed.

Sharing the Light

Jesus sent His disciples, and others, out to minister to the people. This is more than a command; Jesus is giving us an example of how we are to serve Him. We do not need to serve alone. Judas served with Silas (Acts 15:27-32). Barnabas served with Paul (Acts 9:27, Acts 11:26, Acts 12:25). In fact, God set these two aside for specific work (Acts 13:2). Acts 13:16 tells us who Barnabas and Saul shared the gospel with. List them here.

Later in the chapter, Barnabas and Saul are preaching to Jews who become angry. Record their response to the crowd here (Acts 13:44-47).

Verse 49 tells us the outcome. What is it?

Have you ever shared the gospel of Christ with anyone? Were you prepared? Why or why not?

There are steps you can take to be prepared to share the gospel. The first step will likely be to explain why you have faith in Christ. You do not need a heart-gripping testimony, but you should be able to articulate the reasons for your faith. Take some time to prepare your own come-to-Christ story, or state evidence of how Christ has worked in your life.

Have biblical resources available to share with others. This is one reason memorizing Scripture is so important. We do not always have a Bible and concordance available. An example of the steps to share Christ comes from the book of Romans. If you can remember a few verses from this epistle, you can share the gospel with confidence. These verses are easy to memorize. In fact, you may already know them. Record the following verses here, and consider committing them to memory.

Romans 3:10

Romans 3:23

Romans 5:8

Romans 6:23

The most important verse in Romans regarding the plan of salvation is Romans 10:9. Write it here.

Highlight the Scriptures you just transcribed. Sharing any or all of these Scriptures with an unbeliever may lead him or her to a saving faith in our Lord and Savior, Jesus Christ. We are commanded to do just that. "But you are a chosen race, a royal priesthood, a holy nation, a people of His own, so you may proclaim the virtues of the one who called you out of darkness into His marvelous light." 1 Peter 2:9

Write a prayer asking God to give you opportunities
and confidence to share Christ with unbelievers.

Day Five

Creation's Testimony

"Forever since the world was created, people have seen the earth and sky. Through everything God made, they can clearly see His invisible qualities—His eternal power and divine nature. So they have no excuse for not knowing God." Romans 1:20 (NLT)

When you look at the night sky what is revealed to you? Does our Creator communicate with you? Are you listening? Take a short excursion to go look at the stars. During this experience do not talk, simply experience the sights. Let God give you a tour of His glorious creation. Spend a few minutes taking it all in. Allow yourself to be amazed, inspired, and downright overwhelmed with the magnitude and creativity of God. (If you are doing this assignment during daylight hours, log onto www.hubblesite.org/gallery to view images of God's glorious creation.)

What did you experience while gazing at God's handiwork?

We all saw the same thing, but God spoke to each of us in different ways.

List three animals or phenomena from nature that you believe are proof of our Creator God.

1.
2.
3.

Ponder the gift of self-awareness. Consider the brains He has blessed us with. Marvel at our human bodies that cannot be duplicated by any machine. God created us to be special for a purpose. Perhaps you want to understand more? I often turn to other versions of Scripture when I want to learn more detail about a specific passage. Return to Genesis 1. Reprinted below is a selection from the Amplified Version:

> "God said, Let Us [Father, Son, and Holy Spirit] make mankind in Our image, after Our likeness, and let them have complete authority over the fish of the sea, the birds of the air, the [tame] beasts, and over all of the earth, and over everything that creeps upon the earth.
> So God created man in His own image, in the image and likeness of God He created him; male and female He created them.
> And God blessed them and said to them, "Be fruitful, multiply, and fill the earth, and subdue it [using all its vast resources in the service of God and man]; and have dominion over the fish of the sea, the birds of the air, and over every living creature that moves upon the earth.
> And God said, See I have given you every plant yielding seed that is on the face of all the land and every tree with seed in its fruit; you shall have them for food."
>
> Genesis 1:26-29 (AMP)

Circle, or highlight, all the words and phrases describing God's plan for mankind. Could we have done the will of God without the abilities He blessed us with? Why or why not?

The apostle Paul tells us we can see God's invisible qualities all around us (Romans 1:20). We are God's creation, and we interact with God's creation constantly. Each of us must either embrace that fact and live a life surrounded by the light and love Jesus gives us, or we run away from it. We either follow the light, or follow the darkness.

Review Genesis 1:2-2. When did God create Adam and Eve?

What did God make after He created Adam and Eve?

What does the order of creation tell you about God's original plan for mankind?

What does Psalms 139:7-12 tell you about God?

According to this Psalm, where is God?

Creation reveals God to us. He defined the science that made the universe and how our world functions. He had quite a plan in mind when He set creation in motion. God is more than big, He is infinite. God uses His creation as one of many ways to express Himself and to show us who He is. He spoke and water separated from land, and a variety of plants and animals appeared. He created a world full of diverse landscapes, colors, and textures. He created man from dust to become a wonderfully complex and intelligent being, capable of having a relationship with His creator. If our God made all this, surely He has a significant plan for you!

Evidence of God continues to exist all around us. We see the evidence because we see His light. The complex properties of light help us grasp that God is limitless. Light is also simple, it illuminates. Let God's light illuminate your life, so brightly that everyone you meet will be illuminated too.

Do you recall our exercise from week one? We will close with a similar exercise. Fold a blank piece of paper in half. On one side write *How Light Behaves*. On the other side write *How God Behaves*. Brainstorm several responses to each topic and compare your responses.

What similarities and differences do you find?

How does this exercise compare to the exercise in week one, day one?

What evidence of God's behavior do you see in the world today?

We see God and His light in every good thing. Let God's light embrace you as you Follow His Light.

Write a prayer asking God to open your eyes to His work
all around you. Repent that you have ignored God and commit
to following His Light.

"After leaving them, He went up on a mountainside to pray." Mark 6:46b

WEEK EIGHT
AND BEYOND

Reflection

A Place to Pray

Prayer Topics

Reflection

"But Jesus often withdrew to lonely places and prayed." Luke 5:16

John the Baptist made it clear he was not the One; he was making things ready for Christ. Read John 1:8. Based on the words of John the Baptist, what was his purpose?

What is our role?

We are not *the light*, but we should reflect the light of Christ. If we are to reflect God's light properly, we must first take a long, hard look at ourselves.

Mirrors

Mirrors are interesting objects. They do not absorb light; mirrors reflect light and images.[50] What do we do with the light? As always, Scripture gives us the answer. Write Proverbs 27:19 below.

What is in our hearts is reflected in the way we live. Is Christ reflected in you?

How Do Mirrors Work?

All substances reflect, or bounce back, some of the light that falls on them. If the surface is bumpy, the light is reflected in a haphazard manner. What we see appears dull. However, if the reflecting surface is very smooth and polished, light bounces off the surface at the same angle it hits the object. This is called reflection.[51]

When others look at us, what do they see? Do they see a smooth surface reflecting the light of Christ? Instead, do they see something rough or disorderly? Spend some time alone with God to answer these questions, and learn more about yourself. Settle in for some quality time with our Heavenly Father. He wants to hear from you.

A Place and Time

"Pray without ceasing." 1 Thessalonians 5:17 (NASB)

At least two things make it challenging to start a regular prayer routine. First, it is difficult to find a place to pray. Second, it is hard to find a consistent time to pray. A little preparation will help you with both issues.

Finding a Place to Pray

Look for a quiet place, where you will not be disturbed. This might be your kitchen table, if you choose to pray before everyone else in your house is awake. You might use a desk or a comfortable chair in your living room for your prayer spot. You can even use your closet. Ask the Holy Spirit to help you find a place to begin a consistent prayer life. Sometimes it helps to set the mood for prayer. Consider having some of the following prayer aids available to help you focus as you talk to God.

- Cross
- Bibles
- Favorite Scriptures
- Lit candles
- Home fountain
- Soft music
- Devotionals
- Prayers written by others
- Prayer journal or notebook
- Prayer beads
- Fresh flowers

Setting a Time to Pray

Many people will tell you that you should pray first thing in the morning. This may be true for some people, but not for everyone. Many people are more alert later in the day. Draw upon the Holy Spirit to guide you when to pray, and for how long. The key is to give God your best time, and be consistent. Until you get in the habit of regular prayer, you may need to set an alarm, or schedule time to pray.

Once you set a regular prayer time, be protective of that time. It is the most important part of the day.

Prayer Topics

"Then Jesus told his disciples a parable to show them that
they should always pray and not give up." Luke 18:1

Looking in the mirror is not always easy. Sometimes we do not like what we see. We know changes need to be made but we don't know how to start the change process. The following topics are designed to be conversation starters between you and God. Simply discuss one of the following questions with God during your quiet time. There are enough prayer topics listed below to last several weeks. Consider journaling your thoughts in a separate notebook to help you stay focused as you talk to God. This will also help you record God's answers to your prayers.

☐ I am sharing the light and love of God with others.

☐ I trust God.

☐ I believe God speaks to me.

☐ How often have I been moved by faith stories but never tried to grow in my own faith?

☐ I am aware of how blessed I am.

☐ Am I jealous of others blessings?

☐ How can God use me?

☐ Am I obedient to God?

☐ Am I prideful?

☐ Do acquaintances know I am a Christian?

- [ ] When have I been the closest to God?

- [ ] When does God seem most distant?

- [ ] Do I blame God for my problems?

- [ ] God has performed miracles in my life.

- [ ] What changes am I willing to make to grow spiritually?

- [ ] How big is my God?

- [ ] How often do I pray? Is this often enough?

- [ ] I pray for others, not just myself.

- [ ] How often do I read Scripture?

- [ ] What impact does Scripture have on me?

- [ ] What are my favorite passages from Scripture? Why?

- [ ] What is the quality of my prayers?

- [ ] What is my self-talk like?

- [ ] Do I honor the Sabbath?

- [ ] Do I break any of God's commandments frequently?

- [ ] Are there idols in my life?

- [ ] I ask God for His wisdom.

- [ ] Am I thankful? Does my life show gratitude?

- [ ] Do I need to ask for forgiveness?

- [ ] Do I need to forgive others?

- [ ] Have I forgiven myself?

- [ ] Do I express love and compassion?

- [ ] Do I tell people how to improve? Why do I do this?

- [ ] Do I ask for feedback for self-improvement?

- [ ] Do I seek godly counsel?

- [ ] Do I treat my body like the temple of the Lord?

- [ ] What do I value?

- [ ] Do I tithe?

- [ ] Do I volunteer regularly at church or for missions to serve others in God's name?

- [ ] Should I fast? What should I fast from?

- [ ] Am I now, or have I ever been, in spiritual darkness?

- [ ] Have I ever passed on my faith to my children?

- [ ] Have I ever shared Christ with anyone?

- [ ] I go to church because I want to, not out of a sense of duty.

- [ ] If faith was taken out of my life tomorrow morning, how would my life be different?

- [ ] How can I be certain my faith is growing? Can faith be measured?

- [ ] How has my walk with God grown in the past year?

- [ ] The past five years?

- [ ] What three biblical characters would I like to have lunch with and why?

- [ ] What would I ask them?

- [ ] What would they tell me?

- [ ] I want God to change me in this key area:

If you decide not to journal, ask God to help you set up a consistent prayer life.

LEADER'S GUIDE

Leader's Guide

Thank you for facilitating this Bible study. The participants will look to you to guide this study. However, the Lord will lead each participant in His unique way. Nothing is stronger than prayer. Therefore, prior to the study, pray that God will guide you through each week's discussion. Pray for each person who has signed up for the study, asking the Holy Spirit to lead him or her through each assignment and prayer topic.

Be sure to look at the following notes and suggestions a few days before your meeting time. Being prepared is crucial to facilitating a memorable and rewarding Bible study.

Starting a Bible Study

- Publicize the study with your church and community
- Decide on a regular day and time for the group to meet. It is important to honor each person's time commitment. Start promptly and end on time.
- Organize childcare, if needed.
- Determine if snacks and drinks will be provided and who will bring them.
- Obtain enough books for each member of the study to distribute at the opening session.
- Secure a classroom at your church, or a room at a volunteer's home.
- Prepare a comfortable environment for each discussion time. Arrange the seating in a circle so each participant can see all the other participants.
- Before your first session, prepare a sign-up sheet with names, phone numbers and e-mail addresses. Make copies for all participants. Make the participant list, extra Bibles (preferably different versions), and pens or pencils available before each session. If the participants do not know each other, make name tags or name tents. This will facilitate open discussion.
- Open and close each session in prayer.

Session One

- Prior to the session, obtain a piece of poster board to document the group's answers to the Light/God exercise (day one).
- Open in prayer and invite the Holy Spirit to lead the discussion.
- Distribute participant books.
- Have each participant introduce themselves, and state what they hope to glean from this Bible study.
- Discuss the theme of the study.
- Suggest each participant consider a prayer journal. Prayer topics are listed at the end of each daily assignment. The final week also lists many prayer topics.
- As a group, do the week one, day one assignment together. If possible, use a piece of poster board to record the Light/God exercise (day one). Discuss the participant's responses. Keep this poster displayed throughout the study.
- Close in prayer.

Session Two

- Open in prayer and invite the Holy Spirit to lead the discussion.
- Discuss highlights from week one's homework.
- Discuss leaving a godly legacy for our children, grandchildren, and their children.
- Consider doing a Spiritual Gifts Inventory. One is available online at: http://www.spiritualgiftstest.com/.
- Close in prayer.

Session Three

- Open in prayer and invite the Holy Spirit to lead the discussion.
- Discuss highlights from week two's homework.
- If you did not do the Spiritual Gifts Inventory last week, you make consider doing it this week. One is available online at: http://www.spiritualgiftstest.com/.
- Close in prayer.

Session Four

- You might want to secure a nativity scene prior to the lesson, as a visual aid. Display the nativity scene where all participants can view it.
- Open in prayer and invite the Holy Spirit to lead the discussion.
- Discuss the highlights from week three's homework.
- Discuss week three, day four, the Magi's Story. Ask what the participants thought the star of Bethlehem looked like. Relate this discussion to Genesis 1:16.
- Close in prayer.

Session Five

- Open in prayer and invite the Holy Spirit to lead the discussion.
- Discuss highlights from week four's homework.
- Discuss week four, day four, Lightning. Specifically, discuss the light associated around the transfiguration of Christ.
- Close in prayer.

Session Six

- Open in prayer and invite the Holy Spirit to lead the discussion.
- Discuss highlights from week five's homework.
- Discuss week five, day four, Fire. Discuss ways to increase your passion for Christ.
- Close in prayer.

Session Seven

- Prior to the session, obtain a piece of poster board to document the group's answers to the Direct Sun and Artificial Light activity (day five, first paragraph) or the Personal Time exercise (day five).
- Open in prayer and invite the Holy Spirit to lead the discussion.
- Discuss highlights from week six's homework.
- Discuss how the participants responded to the assignments in week six, day five, Direct Sun and Artificial Light activity, or the Personal Time exercise.
- Close in prayer.

Session Eight

- Open in prayer and invite the Holy Spirit to lead the discussion.
- Discuss highlights from week seven's homework.
- If your Bible study meets in the evening and weather permits, arrange for the group to take a walk outside to look at the night sky. Alternately, you could bring a laptop computer and display photos from www.hubblesite.org/gallery. Discuss the vastness of God's creation.
- Encourage participants to continue to pray regularly and show them the sample prayer topics listed in week eight.
- Discuss opportunities to continue your Bible study group, and select another study to use.
- Thank each woman for attending and participating.
- Close in prayer.

Endnotes

1 *Encyclopædia Britannica Online Library Edition*, s.v. "light," accessed July 26, 2013, http://library.eb.com.arlingtontx.idm.oclc.org/eb/article-9110443.

2 Domski, M. (2013). Newton, Sir Isaac. In *Public Libraries*. Retrieved from http://www.worldbookonline.com/pl/infofinder/article?id=ar390180

3 Fairchild, M. D. (2013). Color. In *Public Libraries*. Retrieved from http://www.worldbookonline.com/pl/infofinder/printarticle?id=ar124260&ss=h4

4 Lauber, Patricia, *What Do You see and How Do You See It?* Crown Publishers, New York, NY 1994

5 Domski, M. (2013). Newton, Sir Isaac. In *Public Libraries*. Retrieved from http://www.worldbookonline.com/pl/infofinder/article?id=ar390180

6 *Encyclopædia Britannica Online Library Edition*, s.v. "color," accessed July 26, 2013, http://library.eb.com.arlingtontx.idm.oclc.org/eb/article-9273736.

7 Lauber, Patricia, *What Do You see and How Do You See It?* Crown Publishers, New York, NY 1994

8 Brown, T., & Spilman, A.K. (2013). Light. In *Public Libraries*. Retrieved from http://www.worldbookonline.com/pl/infofinder/article?id=ar323260

9 Wood, Robert, Physics for Kids, 1990, Tab Books, Blue Ridge Summit, PA

10 MacArthur, John, *The MacArthur Bible Commentary* (2005), Thomas Nelson Publishers, Inc., Nashville, TN, Page 1997

11 Pasachoff, J., & Golub, L. (2013). Sun. In *Public Libraries*. Retrieved from http://www.worldbookonline.com/pl/infofinder/article?id=ar539440

12 Ibid.

13 New World Encyclopedia contributors, "Agape," *New World Encyclopedia*, http://www.newworldencyclopedia.org/p/index.php?title=Agape&oldid=793806 (accessed July 27, 2013).

14 Blue Letter Bible. "Dictionary and Word Search for '"*light*"' in the KJV". Blue Letter Bible. 1996-2013. 27 Jul 2013. < http://www.blueletterbible.org/search/translationResults.cfm?Criteria=light&t=KJV >

15 Blue Letter Bible. "Dictionary and Word Search for '*owr (Strong's 216)*". Blue Letter Bible. 1996-2013. 27 Jul 2013. < http:// www.blueletterbible.org/lang/lexicon/lexicon.cfm?Strongs=H216&t=KJV >

16 MacArthur, John, *The MacArthur Bible Commentary* (2005), Thomas Nelson Publishers, Inc., Nashville, TN, Page 8

17 Ibid, Page 926

18 Strong, James, *The New Strong's Complete Dictionary of Bible Words*, 1996, Thomas Nelson Publishers, Inc., Nashville, TN, Page 112

19 Blue Letter Bible. "Dictionary and Word Search for *doxa (Strong's 1391)*". Blue Letter Bible. 1996-2013. 27 Jul 2013. < http:// www.blueletterbible.org/lang/lexicon/lexicon.cfm?Strongs=G1391&t=KJV >

20 MacArthur, John, *The MacArthur Bible Commentary* (2005), Thomas Nelson Publishers, Inc., Nashville, TN, Page 1836

21 Blue Letter Bible. "Dictionary and Word Search for *doxa (Strong's 1391)*". Blue Letter Bible. 1996-2013. 27 Jul 2013. < http:// www.blueletterbible.org/lang/lexicon/lexicon.cfm?Strongs=G1391&t=KJV >

22 Miller, George L., The Shekinah Glory, 2007, Xulon Press, Page 8

23 Ibid, Page 11

24 Rabbi, Dr., Himelstein, Shmuel, *The Jewish Primer,* 1990, The Jerusalem Publishing House, Jerusalem; Facts on File, Inc., New York, NY, pages 27-28

25 Adil, Janeen, *Gods and Goddesses of Ancient Egypt*, 2009, Capstone Press, Mankato, MN

26 *Encyclopædia Britannica Online Library Edition*, s.v. "Thoth," accessed July 27, 2013, http://library.eb.com.arlingtontx.idm.oclc.org/eb/article-9072260.

27 Ask any Boy Scout

28 Starrfield, S. (2013). Southern Cross. In *Public Libraries*. Retrieved from http://www.worldbookonline.com/pl/infofinder/article?id=ar521760

29 Ask any Boy Scout

30 *Encyclopædia Britannica Online Library Edition*, s.v. "light," accessed July 27, 2013, http://library.eb.com.arlingtontx.idm.oclc.org/eb/article-258392.

31 Stille, Darlene, *Manipulating Light, Reflection, Refraction and Absorption*, 2006, Compass Point Books, Minneapolis, MN, page 43

32 World Almanac Library, Understanding the Weather, 2002, Jacques Fortin Publisher, page 36

33 Ibid, page 35

34 MacArthur, John, *The MacArthur Bible Commentary* (2005), Thomas Nelson Publishers, Inc., Nashville, TN, Pages 1127 and 1282

35 Levy, David M., The Tabernacle, Shadows of the Messiah, 1993, The Friends of the Israel Gospel Ministry, Inc., Bellmawr, NJ, page 73

36 *Encyclopædia Britannica Online Library Edition*, s.v. "explosive," accessed July 27, 2013, http://library.eb.com.arlingtontx.idm.oclc.org/eb/article-82363.

37 *Encyclopædia Britannica Online Library Edition*, s.v. "firework," accessed July 27, 2013, http://library.eb.com.arlingtontx.idm.oclc.org/eb/article-9034345.

38 Knapp, Brian, PHD, *Sulfur,* 1996, Atlantic Europe Publishing Co, LTD

39 MacArthur, John, *The MacArthur Bible Commentary* (2005), Thomas Nelson Publishers, Inc., Nashville, TN, Page 891

40 Heelis, R. A. (2013). Aurora. In *Public Libraries*. Retrieved from http://www.worldbookonline.com/pl/infofinder/article?id=ar038160

41 Peterson, D. L. (2013). Fire. In *Public Libraries*. Retrieved from http://www.worldbookonline.com/pl/infofinder/article?id=ar197340

42 MacArthur, John, *The MacArthur Bible Commentary* (2005), Thomas Nelson Publishers, Inc., Nashville, TN, Page 138

43 Ibid, Page 432

44 Ibid, page 432

45 Holman Christian Standard Bible, Study Bible, Holman Bible Publishers, Nashville, TN page 1874

46 Random House College Dictionary, Random House, Inc. New York, 1980

47 *Encyclopædia Britannica Online Library Edition*, s.v. "photosynthesis," accessed July 27, 2013, http://library.eb.com.arlingtontx.idm.oclc.org/eb/article-9108553.

48 Peterson, Eugene, *The Message Translation*, NavPress, Colorado Springs, CO, 2002

49 MacArthur, John, *The MacArthur Bible Commentary* (2005), Thomas Nelson Publishers, Inc., Nashville, TN, Page 1995

50 *Encyclopædia Britannica Online Library Edition*, s.v. "mirror," accessed July 27, 2013, http://library.eb.com.arlingtontx.idm.oclc.org/eb/article-9052946.

51 Darling, David, *Making Light Work*, 1991, The Science of Optics, MacMillan Publishing Co., New York, NY